22.50

T3-BOG-960

THE CELTIC DAWN

THE CELTIC DAWN

A SURVEY OF
THE RENASCENCE IN IRELAND

1889-1916

BY

LLOYD R. MORRIS

NEW YORK
COOPER SQUARE PUBLISHERS, INC.
1970

FERNALD LIBRARY
COLBY-SAWYER COLLEGE
NEW LONDON, N.H. 03257

PR
8750
M6

90901

Originally Published 1917
Published 1970 by Cooper Square Publishers, Inc.
59 Fourth Avenue, New York, N. Y. 10003
Standard Book No. 8154-0359-3
Library of Congress Catalog Card No. 78-132944

Printed in the United States of America

To

PROFESSOR JOHN ERSKINE,
POET, PHILOSOPHER, AND FRIEND,
IN GRATEFUL RECOGNITION

ACKNOWLEDGMENT

A CKNOWLEDGMENT is due to the following publishers for their courtesy in permitting the author to quote from these works: To Messrs. Macmillan for the privilege of quoting from these poems in William Butler Yeats's "Collected Poems:" Rose of the World, He Tells of Perfect Beauty, Into the Twilight, The Moods, He Gives His Beloved Certain Rhymes, The Everlasting Voices; and from these plays, The Shadowy Waters, The King's Threshold, Deirdre, in Yeats's "Plays, Revised and Enlarged"; also from the following essays in "Ideas of Good and Evil," Ireland and the Arts, What Is Popular Poetry?, Symbolism in Poetry, Symbolism in Painting, Magic; and from the Appendix IV of Volume II of the "Poetical Works," and from the Preface to "Plays for An Irish Theater."

To Messrs. John Lane for the privilege of quoting the following poems by A. E., from "Homeward Songs by the Way," and "The Earth Breath"; Breaghy, The Memory of Earth, The

Great Breath, Dusk, Symbolism, Dust, The Man and the Angel, Reconciliation, The Twilight of Earth, Illusion. To Messrs. Macmillan for the privilege of quoting from "Imaginations and Reveries," passages from these essays, The Renewal of Youth, Ideals of the New Rural Society.

To Messrs. John W. Luce and Co., for permission to quote from the Prefaces of "The Tinker's Wedding" and "The Playboy of the Western World," by J. M. Synge, and from The Vagrants of Wicklow, in "In Wicklow and West Kerry."

To Messrs. Duffield and Co., for permission to quote the poem To My Best Friend, from "Songs of the Fields," by Francis Ledwidge; and to them and to Mrs. Elizabeth Sharp for permission to quote two poems, The Vision, and Day and Night, from the "Collected Works of Fiona Macleod," and a passage from a letter to Fiona Macleod by A. E. in Mrs. Sharp's "William Sharp: A Memoir."

To Messrs. Macmillan for permission to quote from "The Demigods" by James Stephens, and Mystic and Cavalier and Harmonies from the "Collected Poems of Lionel Johnson."

To Mr. Mitchell Kennerley for permission to quote from an article, The Irish Dramatist and

the Irish People, by St. John G. Ervine in "The
Forum" of June, 1914. To "The Century Magazine" for permission to quote from The Old
Woman's Money, by James Stephens in "The
Century" for May, 1915. To "Pearson's Magazine" for permission to quote from The Fight
of the Irish Farmers, by Charles Edward Russell,
in "Pearson's Magazine" of September, 1915.

To Messrs. Henry Holt and Co., for permission
to reprint "The Plougher" from Padraic Colum's
"Wild Earth."

LLOYD R. MORRIS.

FOREWORD

"THE Celtic Dawn" is a study of the several movements which, although having their foundation in a single consciously expressed philosophy, have labored in widely varied fields to produce a new social synthesis in contemporary Ireland. I have found five of these to be of major importance as forces contributing toward this result. These five movements are those which have been concerned with literature, the drama, with the revival of Gaelic as the language of daily speech, with economic and social reform, and with political thought. Although the Irish literary and dramatic renascence has given rise to a great deal of critical and explanatory writing, and the recent insurrection has turned the attention of many to the political aspirations and social ideals of the new Ireland, I know of no other attempt to consider these various movements in their relation to each other, and to consider them as collectively laboring at the reconstruction of Irish life. That "The Celtic Dawn" has chosen this field as its province must constitute its claim upon the attention of the reader.

I anticipate a further question. Why, the reader may ask, should Ireland be of interest to the general public? For four reasons which may be briefly enumerated. Because at the present moment the "Irish question" is the most important internal problem that the British Empire has to solve. Because in the economic organization of agrarian industries Irish economists have evolved and put into actual practice a philosophy the application of which to the economic life of our own rural communities has only begun to be appreciated. Because the Irish literary and dramatic movement is the most vital contribution that has been made to contemporary English literature. And, finally, because Ireland, although her government was mismanaged from Westminster, and her economic life was ruined by the tinkering of politicians who did not understand her problems, although thirty years ago her intellectual life was in a state of stagnation, has discovered in the five movements I have spoken of the means of preserving her national spirit, of reorganizing her economic life, of producing a literature of special importance to the world in the quality of its spiritual content, and of realizing the social synthesis of which this volume is a study.

My obligations in the preparation of this book
have been many. First and foremost to my mother
and my father, who have carefully read each
chapter as it has been written and rewritten.
My debt to Professor John Erskine of Columbia
University can only be acknowledged, never
repaid. He, too, read the book and aided me
greatly by the clarity of his vision and the pene-
tration of his suggestions for its improvement.
To Doctor H. W. L. Dana of Columbia University and to Mr. Maurice L. Firuski I am indebted
for bringing to my attention two volumes that
might otherwise have escaped notice.

Finally, I shall always treasure the memory
of an illuminating visit to Mr. George W. Russell,
"A. E.," in his charming home in Rathgar, Dublin.
There, surrounded by beautiful pictures of his
own painting, I had the inestimable privilege of
coming into contact with the most vital and most
versatile mind in contemporary Ireland, that of
the distinguished poet, mystic, philosopher, artist,
economist and critic, the acknowledged leader
of the renascence.

LLOYD R. MORRIS.

NEW YORK CITY,
  August, 1916.

TABLE OF CONTENTS

CHAPTER I

CHAPTER II

CHAPTER III

CHAPTER IV

Origin of the dramatic movement. The plays of
Yeats. His theory of tragedy and comedy. The
qualities of his poetic drama. George Moore.
Edward Martyn and the "intellectual drama."
Lady Gregory and the folk-play. Douglas Hyde
and A. E. John Millington Synge. The theme
of his art. His theories of the art of the playwright.
His conception of character. His poetry. His use of

THE CELTIC DAWN

THE CELTIC DAWN

CHAPTER I

THE FORCES AT WORK

MOST people in America have come to think of the Irish renascence as a movement born of the early political enthusiasms of William Butler Yeats, taking from him the direction of its thought, laboring at first in verse and in the revival of a moribund language, and later in the creation of a body of dramatic material for the use of a little theater in Dublin. They have come to think of its work as a purely literary phenomenon characterized by peculiar tendencies in form and in substance, the product of an intellectual aristocracy somewhat removed from life and its problems. This conception, however, does not recognize the fact that the renascence in Ireland is the expression of a social synthesis, having its foundations in political and social history, concerned as much with intellectual emancipation and economic progress as it is with the art by which it is most widely known. An intimate connection

I

exists between the various phases of the movement, literary, dramatic, economic and social, for
all of them have been inspired by a common aim,
the reconstruction of Irish life, and it is my purpose to make evident the realization of that aim
in the principal fields of activity which it has per-
vaded. For the present, however, it will suffice to
briefly trace the course of literature in Ireland during
the century immediately preceding the renascence.

The end of the seventeenth century witnessed
the final and complete disintegration of the once
powerful bardic order, and the making of verses
in the native tongue was relegated to a few scat-
tered individuals, chiefly in Munster, and to the
bulk of the peasantry, who, having not then lost
command of the Gaelic, were enabled to sing of
their sorrow, their hopes and their loves and form
a body of folk-poetry which has only within com-
paratively recent years been made the subject of
study and collection. Until the beginning of the
nineteenth century that part of Ireland to which
English was the native language possessed no distinctively national literature. With Thomas
Moore, whose lyrics were written for Irish music,
and with Maria Edgeworth, whose novels are the
first expression in prose of an interest in the life

of the Irish peasant, a start had been made in the creation of a distinctively national literature. Following Moore came a few translators from the Irish, chief among them J. J. Callanan, and these were, in turn, followed by the poets of "Young Ireland." "Young Ireland" was the name chosen by the group of young intellectuals who followed O'Connell until the fatal day at Clontarf when the veteran leader gave the signal to disband, and all hope of a successful revolution was lost. After the downfall of O'Connell's theory of "agitation within the law," "Young Ireland" split into two parties, one of which, that led by John Mitchel, declared themselves in favor of an immediate revolution, while the other, of which Thomas Davis was the chief leader, attempted a propaganda of moral and intellectual reform. Davis, himself a poet of no mean ability, was essentially a propagandist, and founded a paper, "The Nation," in which appeared the verse and prose to which his political philosophy gave birth. The most important contributors to "The Nation," aside from Davis himself, were James Clarence Mangan and Edward Walsh. Mangan's work, like that of Coleridge, to whom he bears some resemblance, is characterized by a powerful and tortured imagi-

nation and great lyric beauty, and he perhaps is
the most truly poetic of all the "Young Ireland"
poets. Edward Walsh, who was a village school-
master, wrote many finely poetic translations from
the Gaelic, and "Speranza," who later became
known as Lady William Wilde, wrote some verse
of merit, and much stirring prose. In the meanwhile, John Mitchel had founded "The United
Irishman" and had commenced to preach the
doctrine of blood and iron that culminated in
his imprisonment and the disastrous revolution
of 1848. His prison sentence resulted in the
composition of his "Jail Journal," a book that
even today exercises a profound effect on political
thought in Ireland. The revolution was succeeded
by the great famine of 1849, the coercion acts
passed by the English government, the tremen-
dous emigration to America, and finally, by the
rise of the Fenian party. The Fenian movement
took up the doctrines of John Mitchel, and, although materially it was a failure, it exercised a
wide influence on subsequent political reform.
Its literary productivity was small, the verse of
Charles Kickham and of Ellen O'Leary, the sister
of the revolutionist John O'Leary, being most
fairly representative, verse which was less fiery

than that of "Young Ireland," and less hopeful
in its outlook. During the period of Fenianism
Sir Samuel Ferguson, William Allingham, and
Aubrey de Vere were publishing poetry that
found none of its inspiration in politics. Allingham was the poet of life in the West, a lyricist of
subtle charm and wistful beauty, a poet of delicate
mood and a melancholy nature. Ferguson drew
for his material on the old bardic tradition, and
was successful principally in depicting action
and the clash of high passions, while Aubrey de
Vere wrote verse that was meditative and religious,
and was influenced equally by Ireland, the Catholic tradition, and Wordsworth. In 1889, the year
in which both Allingham and Ellen O'Leary died,
William Butler Yeats published his "Wanderings
of Oisin" and Douglas Hyde his "Leabhar Sgeuluigheachta" (A Book of Gaelic Stories) and it is
from the publication of these two books that both
the revival of Gaelic and the revival of Irish literature written in English date.[1]

[1] For a discussion of the history of "Young Ireland" and
Fenianism, see "Contemporary Ireland," by L. Paul-Dubois,
Maunsel and Co., Dublin, 1911; Historical Introduction,
Chap. II, pp. 65–79. For a brief discussion of the poetry of
the period, see "A Book of Irish Verse," ed. W. B. Yeats,
3d ed. Methuen, London, 1911.

The fundamental ideas of Yeats and Hyde were identical in purpose. Yeats, because of his early association with a "Young Ireland" group, followed the theories of Davis, and planned to create a literature in English which would express the national consciousness in Ireland, which would throw Irish thought back upon its own tradition and thus release it from an intellectual dependence upon England. Hyde proceeded upon the theory that the essence of nationality is contained in language, and, believing that the soul of a nation is expressed in its living speech as well as in its literature and in its art, he devoted his energies to reviving the ancient and rapidly dying speech of the people, and to giving Ireland a modern literature in her own tongue. An analogy may be traced between the literary activity that ensued, and the history of Elizabethan literature. Both were the fulfillment of a desire for a purely national art; in both instances creative activity was prefaced and accompanied by critical discussion dealing with the general theory of poetry and with the medium of expression to be employed; finally, the creative intelligence of both periods was directed toward poetry, the drama, and, in its latest development, the novel.

During the period of propaganda that was later to result in a wide artistic productivity, certain social forces likewise made themselves manifest. First and foremost of these were the efforts made to ameliorate the conditions of living among the peasantry. These efforts assumed two general tendencies; one was directed toward the rehabilitation of cottage crafts and of the arts formerly cultivated by the peasantry; the other was committed to the furtherance of economic and agrarian reform and has had a far reaching effect not only upon public policy but also upon the solution of the economic problems peculiar to a country whose resources are mainly agricultural, and whose government has been as patently mismanaged as that of Ireland.

In their operation, all these various forces, both artistic and social, have interacted, and often the boundaries between them have become indistinguishable, but for the purpose of this essay it has been deemed more expedient to deal first with the artistic, and then with the social phases. In the field of art the more clearly indicated divisions are criticism and the revival of Gaelic, poetry, the drama, and the novel. And since it is in the critical writing of the movement that its most fundamental problems appear, the critical theories involved provide the most favorable foundations for a survey of the Celtic renascence in the arts.

CHAPTER II

THE problems with which the criticism of the Irish renascence has been mostly profitably concerned are those which have arisen in the development of a native literature and drama, and chief among them in the degree of its influence on subsequent creative art has been the discussion of expression, or, as it may more conveniently be termed, the problem of language. A prior controversy concerning the relative values of nationality and cosmopolitanism in art served to delimit three points of view in regard to language, and employed the energies of three men, George W. Russell, William Butler Yeats and John Eglinton, who, with Doctor Douglas Hyde, may be said to control the ideas of the Irish revival.

The propaganda for the revival of the Gaelic language which was instituted by Douglas Hyde with the publication, in 1889, of "Leabhar Sgeuluigheachta" (A Book of Gaelic Stories), resulted

four years later in the organization of the Gaelic
League, a non-political body having as its purpose the rehabilitation of the native language
and arts, and the creation of a modern literature
in Irish. To this end Doctor Hyde published, in
1894, his "Love Songs of Connacht," a volume
of poems in Irish with an accompanying translation into the literal English equivalent, and this
translation marks the first use of the Anglo-Irish
peasant dialect as a medium of artistic expression.
In the meanwhile Yeats, who in 1889 had published "The Wanderings of Oisin," conceived the
project of creating a literature that would adequately express the Celtic consciousness in the
English language, and in the collection of folk-lore
and folk-history with which he had busied himself, he had come upon the peasant dialect to
which Doctor Hyde had given the first literary
usage, and allured by the wealth and the poetry
of its expression, advocated its use in literature.

The soul of Ireland, it seemed to Yeats, was to
be found in its tradition, in its history, in its folk-
legends, the consciousness of which has had its
psychological influence in two qualities that he
deems peculiar to the Irish people, the tense ardor
of patriotism manifested in their protracted

struggle for political independence, and the half pagan, half Christian belief in the reality of an unseen world which had made possible the co-existence of both the faery realm and Catholic theology. Like Thomas Davis, whose theories he has in a measure inherited, Yeats's nationalism was directed rather toward an intellectual and moral revolution than toward one purely political in its nature; he desired a spiritual renascence, and he believed that it could be achieved by employing art as a medium, and, therefore, by creating an art having its foundation in the soul of the race. "I would have Ireland," he has written, "recreate the ancient arts, the arts as they were understood in Judea, in India, in Scandinavia, in Greece and Rome, in every ancient land; as they were understood when they moved a whole people and not a few people who have grown up in a leisure class and made this understanding their business."[1] In literature this art was to find

[1] Quoted from "Ireland and the Arts," in "Ideas of Good and Evil," Collected Works, Vol. VI, A. H. Bullen, London, 1908. The book is a subtle interpretation of Yeats's point of view, and will be drawn on more fully in a later section; three essays are especially important in understanding the author's critical outlook, that quoted above, "The Celtic Element in Literature," and "The Autumn of the Body."

its language in the rich idiom of the peasantry
of the west, a doctrine in which Yeats has
more lately been joined by a younger poet
and critic, Thomas MacDonagh. The thesis
of their contention is that modern English, the
English of contemporary literature, is essentially
an impoverished language incapable of directly
expressing thought, for it has become practically
impossible for the writer to distinguish between
the substance of his thought and the conventional
phrase which is its code in expression, although
the connotation is sufficiently indirect to render
a misinterpretation by his reader an equal possibility.[1] They view English as a language that
has lost its vitality, as an imperfect algebra of
thought, as merely an approximation in expression of the intellectual substance. Therefore
they counsel the use of Anglo-Irish, which, since
it is a colloquial language and not a literary, is
the direct expression of experience, and has never
been standardized in its suggestiveness, nor viti-
ated in its power to adequately reflect with equal

[1] See "The Irish Review" for May, 1914, "Criticism and
Irish Poetry" by Thomas MacDonagh, and same, June, 1914,
"Language and Literature in Ireland." MacDonagh was
executed in Dublin by the military authorities after the insurrection of April, 1916.

richness of connotation the concreteness of life
and the abstraction of thought. They find the
historical justification of their theory in the fact
that Anglo-Irish is a product of the fusion of
Elizabethan English with the rough old mold of
the Gaelic tongue, and as such is the medium of
expression most purely adapted to the Celtic
mind and to Celtic life.

Opposed to the theory of the language movement stands W. K. Magee, better known as "John
Eglinton," author of the most acute criticism
that the Celtic renascence has yet inspired, a
writer whose trenchant, powerful style and rugged
thought place him among the most valuable of
contemporary essayists, although the service that
he has rendered to the movement has often been
esteemed but a disservice.[1] Eglinton's thesis is
that the essential spirit of nationality is born of
the peasantry, but that historically, both lan-

[1] The writings of John Eglinton are: "Two Essays on the
Remnant," 1896, "Pebbles from a Brook," 1901, "Bards and
Saints,"1906, Tower Press Booklets, Series I, No. 5, Maunsel
& Co., Dublin. "Some Literary Ideals in Ireland," London:
Fisher Unwin, 1899. Also see "Dana" a discontinued magazine of which he was editor. Eglinton is one of the most
original thinkers in Ireland today, and his influence is ex-
tremely important in the development of thought in contemporary Ireland.

guage and literature have been imposed by a
superior culture.   And in "Bards and Saints" he
proves conclusively that the aspiration of nationality was not an outgrowth of peasant thought
in Ireland, but came from the Anglo-Irish mind,
which took no cognisance of the true national
nucleus, the peasant.   Political thought later
relegated the idea of nationality to the peasant
nucleus, which had the benefit neither of a superior culture that had been imposed on it from
without, nor of a native and indigenous culture or
spiritual life to give it individuality.   It is in a
thought movement rather than in a language
movement, he claims, that the spirit of nationality
proclaims itself, and in the revival of an essentially
moribund language he finds only the occasion for
a schism in what appears to him to be the first
dawn of a truly national consciousness in Ireland.
And he is perhaps the only writer who has pointed
out the futility of attempting to dispense with the
accumulated culture of centuries of English intellectual development in order to create a literature written in a language that "has never undergone a spiritual discipline, and still retains a rude
flavour as of a language which has never been
properly to school."   His antagonism to Yeats's

theory of the expression of nationality in art has been equally determined. In an essay on "The De-Davisation of Irish Literature" he distinguishes between literature, which is the faithful record of an individual impression, and rhetoric, which is the art of persuasion directed to a particular audience, and journalism, which, at its best, is a fusion of both. That Davis was a brilliant journalist, he claims is evident in the fact that he succeeded in inspiring subsequent Irish national literature with his theory, which was that literature was to be "not the interpretation of the soul of a people, still less the emancipation of the national mind by means of individual utterance, but—no doubt a very good thing—the expression of such sentiments as help to exalt an Irishman's notions of the excellence and importance of the race to which he belongs." Mitchel, on the other hand, wrote his "Jail Journal" under the influence of an overmastering desire for self expression, and without thought of an audience, and succeeded in producing not only literature, but literature which for the first time interpreted, perhaps unconsciously, the spirit of Irish nationality. "It must be confessed," he goes on to say, and this passage contains the core of his thought, "that

when Anglo-Irish literature has brought us at
least so far as the literary integrity and hearty
directness of John Mitchel, it seems a pity if the
'Language Movement' is to transport literature
in this country back again to the point where the
good Davis left it, to that region, which has now
become somewhat insipid, in which all private
differences are sunk, and in which the Irishman
has to speak in his national rather than in his
human capacity. For the questions which divide
household and nation against themselves, religious, political, fundamental questions, these are
the questions in respect to which the literary man
must have the license of a prophet; it is these
which he looks on as his peculiar region; it is these
upon which literature, more than any other
agency, can hope to shed some light. Literature
must be as free as the elements; if that is to be
cosmopolitan it must be cosmopolitan." The
theories of Eglinton, Yeats and Hyde do not
differ in the fundamental purpose of achieving
an intellectual and artistic emancipation, but in
the method by which it may be attained. Yeats
and Hyde represent the two divisions of nationalism in art, the one advocating the use of Anglo-
Irish, the other, of Gaelic, while Eglinton stands

for the broader cosmopolitan of thought that for the past century has been characteristic of European art. The influence of Eglinton is apparent in the work of Frederick Ryan, whose "Criticism and Courage" is a demonstration of the necessity of intellectual freedom in Ireland as an essential in the development of national progress, and is chiefly directed against the domination over thought exercised by the clerical dogma and tradition that constitutes the reactionary element in Irish public consciousness. On the other hand, the nationalist theory of art has been upheld by no less able critic than George W. Russell, whose genius is confined to no one field, and who has contributed under the pseudonym of "A. E." to poetry, to the drama, to painting and to social economy. His statement of the conception of nationalism in art is made in the little volume "Irish Essays," and is not limited by allegiance to either of the two language movements. He views nationality less as a political than a spiritual force creating ideals that have never had philosophic definition or supreme expression in literature, and believes that those writers who give to the vague the expression that it demands are evolving not only a national literature, but the soul of a nation as well.

The influence of the theory of nationalism in art has, however, not been entirely directed toward the selection of subject; the interest in expression which was productive of the literary usage of peasant idiom has been one of its most potent characteristics, and this interest, apart from its obvious utility to a distinctively national art, depended upon an esthetics that has had its most complete definition in the critical writing of Yeats. In considering the esthetic theories of Yeats it must not be forgotten that the predominating feeling of his verse is lyrical, even in his long poem, "The Wandering of Oisin" and in his later dramatic writing, and that the essence of a lyric lies in the expression of mood or of an emotion which, far from being controlled by the poet, is so powerful and so compelling that, for the moment, the emotion controls the man. In this respect lyricism is the direct antithesis of prose, which, at its purest, is the complete control of expression by intellect. The statement which most clearly enunciates Yeats's position in criticism is contained in a brief summary of the principles of the Abbey Theater.[1] "Before men read," he has

[1] Cited from "The Work of the National Theatre Society at the Abbey Theatre, Dublin; A Statement of Principles."

written, "the ear and the tongue were subtle, and delighted one another with the little tunes that were in words. . . . They loved language, and all literature was then, whether in the mouth of minstrels, players, or singers, but the perfection of an art that everybody practised, a flower from the stem of life." And in another passage he has written, "Without fine words there is no literature." With the subjugation of literature to print, beautiful language decayed, for the appeal to the ear had been forgotten, and the beauty of words, depending, as it does, upon utterance by the voice, lost the quality of its allusion, and words became merely the counters of thought. The art that he desired to create was to come out of life, expressing those emotions that, evoking images of beauty, are in themselves beautiful, and for this he deemed the language of ordinary use impossible, while the language of poetry expressed little relation to life. Therefore he felt it necessary to create a style, the elements of which he found in a language that came out of life but that had not been corrupted by print, the dialect of the

Appendix IV in Vol. II of "The Poetical Works of William Butler Yeats," The Macmillan Company, New York, 1914.

peasants, which had lost nothing of the picturesque allusion or the vocable beauty with which the language of poetry had, in a former day, been pregnant. This preoccupation with style is innate not only in the work of Yeats but also in that of the two other writers who have been most intimately associated with him, John Millington Synge and Lady Gregory. Closely related to it, and in part dependent upon it is the desire to substitute the Irish for the English tradition in the poetry of the Celtic renascence. Symbols derive their connotation from the associations that they evoke, and those things which, in the genesis of a long tradition, have become true symbols are always those which express the perfection of the quality of which they are the type. Symbolism presupposes an acquaintance with the tradition of which it is born, a tradition, whether written or unwritten, that is a cumulative record of life, and therefore Yeats, in his search for a style directly expressive of life, employed one that is rich in symbol, and in this, also, he has been followed by Synge and by Lady Gregory, who, if they are not strictly symbolists, have built up a style that is largely metaphorical.[1] This lyrical,

[1] These theories are stated for the most part in " Ideas of

or as some critics prefer to term it, realistic, immediacy of art, that finds its expression in symbol, is characteristic not alone of Yeats and the group that followed him, but of certain Irish writers upon whom he has had no influence, and of a group of continental writers, of whom the most famous is Maurice Maeterlinck.

The tradition presupposed by the symbolists in Ireland had received its first evaluation in modern criticism from Renan, in his "Poetry of the Celtic Races" in 1859, and from Arnold, in his essay "On the Study of Celtic Literature" in 1865. German scholarship, with its customary thoroughness, devoted itself to research and the redaction of texts, while in Ireland Standish O'Grady and Doctor P. W. Joyce prepared the legends for subsequent poetic use, and before them Petrie and Sir William Wilde had interested themselves in the study of the decaying language and customs of the Gael. In France, likewise, the study of Gaelic, and especially of the Breton dialect, prospered; courses in the language were given at the College de France, the Revue Celtique had been founded, and Irish literary so-

Good and Evil," in the essays on "The Symbolism of Painting" and "The Symbolism of Poetry."

cieties discussed literature and politics in a desultory but not unprofitable manner. The first attempt to give Ireland a modern literature in her own language came, as has been said, with the publication of Douglas Hyde's first book, in 1889. In 1893 he founded the Gaelic League, which became the most potent factor in urging the renascence of Irish in Ireland, and which, likewise, has been of inestimable service to the renascence of Irish literature in English. The League is a non-political, non-sectarian body; its chief concern is the propagation of Irish as a spoken and as a literary language and the creation of a literature embodying a sufficiently close spiritual relation to the life of the people to be readily understood by them. With the growth of a popular interest in the language, the League has turned its attention to the revival of the ancient arts, among them the cottage crafts and the communal arts of singing, dancing, and narration, for which there are frequent competitions. The chief service of the League to literature has been the recovery of the tradition long hidden both in folk-lore and in the undeciphered manuscripts of old Gaelic poetry, which have been rescued, in great part, from oblivion by Professor Kuno Meyer, whose translations are an enduring monument to his philological attainment and to the cherishing care with which he has rendered the old bardic feeling in lucid and readable English.   The impetus given to a latent interest in the old legends and the cultivation of the tradition and culture of the race through the medium of language have resulted in an increased emphasis upon those tendencies of the Celtic mind which distinguish it from the Anglo-Saxon, into which it had been in danger of becoming absorbed, and in the preparation of material upon which that mind, when it had attained the consciousness of self perequisite to its functioning in art, could exercise its creative energies.

The general critical theories have developed certain well defined tendencies traceable in the subsequent development of creative art in Ireland. First in importance is the creation of a national culture through literature embodying the ideals and the spirit of the race.   This literature, essentially democratic in its aim, is characterized by a desire to approach life in its simplest and most truthful terms and to deal with its essence rather than with its external manifestations.   In the matter of expression there have been three divergent views, one of which claims precedence for

Gaelic, the other for English, and the third for the present dialect, or Anglo-Irish, as the language in which the Celtic mind and the Celtic soul achieve their fullest expression. And, finally, there has been the interest in language for its own beauty; in the revival of the Celtic tradition, folk-lore and legend, and, born, perhaps, of this interest, the view of life which dismisses that which we ordinarily call reality as externality, and loses itself in the spirit, finding its expression in symbol.

CHAPTER III

POETRY was the first of the literary forms to attract the writers of the Celtic renascence, and this, perhaps, for two reasons; the literature which had come out of both ancient and modern Ireland had been, in the main, poetic, and the genesis of the Celtic literary movement was conceived in the attempt to write popular poetry of literary merit. For the rest, poetry, although the drama has claimed many of its priesthood, has given to Ireland what may well be its most enduring art.

For many of the poets of contemporary Ireland poetry has been the voice of social protest, for many it has been a philosophy or an art passionately cherished, a tapestry woven on the loom of beauty; to one at least it has been that which Plato held it, the expression of a soul inspired by the breath of the gods. A visionary and a mystic, A. E. believes in the validity of his inspiration, and although his is the most vivid person-

25

ality in Ireland today, his verse is curiously impersonal, and even though there is in it the lyric
enthusiasm of the soul become one with the infinite and eternal oversoul, this enthusiasm is cold,
pure, unsensuous. Poetry is to him highly serious, for it is the ritual of his religion, and it is
holy, for its inspiration is the breath of divinity.
A deliberate estheticism plays no part either in his
verse or in his painting, for he does not accept the
standards of art as the conditioning factor of the
expression of the spirit that in itself is the source of
all creative activity. To comprehend his view of
life one must return by way of Blake and Jacob
Boehme, by way of Swedenborg and Crashaw and
Santa Teresa to the neoplatonists of Alexandria, to
Plato himself, and to the sacred books of the east;
for his philosophy of life is not a product of Ireland,
although it has profoundly influenced the literature
that we are considering. It is, however, a product
of the conflict between the rational and intuitional
explanations of the world, between the despotism
of fact and the revelation of a spiritual order beside
which fact sinks into insignificance, which has been
characteristic, in one form or another, of every
period of thought in man's intellectual history.

Plato, it will be remembered, explained the

vision of the mystic by the beautiful fable of the
heavenly chariot ride of the unborn soul, and in
his declaration that inspiration is a divine madness
attained by those who have kept the soul sensitive
to beauty.   A similar belief underlies A. E.'s reaction to life.

With the Brahmins and with Plato, he holds
that the life of the soul is cyclic, that its physical
birth and rebirth is but the condition of a pil-
grimage from the eternal to the eternal, and that
the spiritual memories of the eternal are the motivating forces of physical life. This has found
definite expression in the preface to his "Homeward: Songs by the Way": (1894) "I move among
men and places, and in living I learned the truth
at last.   I know I am a spirit, and that I went
forth in old time from the self-ancestral to labours
yet unaccomplished; but filled ever and again with
homesickness I made these songs by the way."
Spiritual memory was explained by Plato as the
recollection of the visions of those Ideas which
were seen by the soul in its heavenly ride; with
A. E. this conception has been fused with the
doctrine of ancestral memory, a recapitulation of
the evolution of race consciousness that is present,
subconsciously, in all individuals, a doctrine that

has been important in the point of view of two
other poets, W. B. Yeats, and "Fiona Macleod."
To Plato, beauty consisted in the suggestion of
immortality, and it is this idea of beauty that has
been present not alone in the verse of Crashaw and
Blake, who were mystics, but also in that of
Spenser, Milton and Wordsworth, who were Pla-
tonists, though not essentially of a mystic nature.
It is to Wordsworth, among all the English poets,
however, that A. E. is most closely related, and
the bond that is between them lies chiefly in their
view of nature.

To Wordsworth and to A. E., and to Emerson,
with whom A. E. has often been compared, the
suggestion of immortality that is beauty has been
inspired most frequently by nature, and nature to
them has been the symbol of a universal spirit of
which man realizes himself a part in the rare moments of ecstasy that are true vision.   Earthly
beauty, to the man whose soul is sensitive to all
the subtle influences of form and color, is but
the suggestion of a beauty more spiritual, visual-
ized, perhaps, but in a vague dream of some other
self, in a moment when the soul has had its life
apart.   In its vision of this beauty the soul is
bound by the senses and their experience of what

we know as life, and always it clothes the formless essence of spiritual beauty in the symbol of a beauty that is earthly but that is the most perfect that the senses know, for the imagination is but memory, and all art and all knowledge are born of memory alone.   Art, because it seeks the soul through the emotions, and the emotions through the senses, has found its symbols in the world of sensation; but spiritual beauty, being impalpable, finds its expression equally in ideas, and the contribution of our day to the history of beauty has been in our recognition of the poetry of science, and the beauty of abstract ideas.   And to the mystic the laws of science are but the symbolic expression of spiritual law, as earthly beauty is but the suggestion of the beauty of the soul of the world, that is revealed to the intuition in a moment of exaltation that is called inspired. It is this pantheism, this quest of the soul for unity with the spirit of life, that makes A. E., as it did Wordsworth, essentially a poet of nature, although nature is but the symbol of that spirit and the inspiration of the mood of ecstasy.

Of this mood informed of ecstasy, he has written in a poem called "Breaghy":

"When twilight flutters the mountains over,
  The faery lights from the earth unfold:
  And over the caves enchanted hover
  The giant heroes and gods of old.
  The bird of aether its flaming pinions
  Waves over earth the whole night long:
  The stars drop down in their blue dominions
  To hymn together their choral song.
  The child of earth in his heart grows burning,
  Mad for the night and the deep unknown:
  His alien flame in a dream returning
  Seats itself on the ancient throne.
  When twilight over the mountains fluttered,
  And night with its starry millions came,
  I too had dreams: the songs I have uttered
  Come from this heart that was touched by the flame."

And he has written of symbolism thus:

"Now when the spirit in us wakes and broods,
  Filled with home yearnings, drowsily it flings
  From its deep heart high dreams and mystic moods,
  Mixed with the memory of the loved earth things:
  Clothing the vast with a familiar face;
  Reaching its right hand forth to greet the starry race.

"Wondrously near and clear the great warm fires
  Stare from the blue; so shows the cottage light
  To the field labourer whose heart desires
  The old folk by the nook, the welcome bright
  From the house-wife long parted from at dawn—
  So the star villages in God's great depths withdrawn.

"Nearer to Thee, not by delusion led,
  Though there no house fires burn nor bright eyes gaze:
  We rise, but by the symbol charioted,
  Through loved things rising up to Love's own ways:
  By these the soul unto the vast has wings
  And sets the seal celestial on all mortal things."

His relations with nature are set forth in a little poem entitled "Dust," one of the most profound poetic expressions in literature of a philosophy of the spirit.

"I heard them in their sadness say,
  'The earth rebukes the thought of God;
  We are but embers wrapped in clay
  A little nobler than the sod.'

"But I have touched the lips of clay,
  Mother, thy rudest sod to me
  Is thrilled with fire of hidden day,
  And haunted by all mystery."

Were it not for the impelling quest of the spiritual life, A. E. could perhaps have been content, as many poets have been content, to express the beauty of nature for the sake of that beauty itself, to express with a frank paganism the joy of material things in the adventure of life, to find, in what to him is symbol, the very essence of being. There are, in his verse, many indications that

such might have been the case, and these lie in
the rare but exquisite descriptions of external nature, or, more often, of the opalescent twilight sky
as the charioting symbols. "The Memory of
Earth" is a striking example:

> "In the wet dusk silver sweet,
>   Down the violet scented ways,
>   As I moved with quiet feet
>   I was met by mighty days.
>
> "On the hedge the hanging dew
>   Glassed the eve and stars and skies;
>   While I gazed a madness grew
>   Into thundered battle cries.
>
> "Where the hawthorn glimmered white,
>   Flashed the spear and fell the stroke—
>   Ah, what faces pale and bright
>   Where the dazzling battle broke!
>
> "There a hero-hearted queen
>   With young beauty lit the van:
>   Gone! the darkness flowed between
>   All the ancient wars of man.
>
> "While I paced the valley's gloom
>   Where the rabbits pattered near,
>   Shone a temple and a tomb
>   With the legend carven clear:

> "'Time put by a myriad fates
>   That her day might dawn in glory;
> Death made wide a million gates
>   So to close her tragic story.'"

And "The Great Breath" is another:

> "Its edges foamed with amethyst and rose,
>   Withers once more the old blue flower of day:
> There where the ether like a diamond glows
>   Its petals fade away.

> "A shadowy tumult stirs the dusky air;
>   Sparkle the delicate dews, the distant snows;
> The great deep thrills, for through it everywhere
>   The breath of beauty blows.

> "I saw how all the trembling ages past,
>   Moulded to her by deep and deeper breath,
> Neared to the hour when beauty breathes her last
>   And knows herself in death."

Or these lines of "Dusk:"

> "Dusk wraps the village in its dim caress;
>   Each chimney's vapour, like a thin grey rod,
> Mounting aloft through miles of quietness,
>   Pillars the skies of God.

> "Far up they break or seem to break their line,
>   Mingling their nebulous crests that bow and nod
> Under the light of those fierce stars that shine
>   Out of the calm of God.

.   .   .   .

FERNALD LIBRARY
COLBY-SAWYER COLLEGE
NEW LONDON, N.H. 03257

90901

"Only in clouds and dreams I felt those souls
  In the abyss, each fire hid in its clod;
  From which in clouds and dreams the spirit rolls
    Into the vast of God."

But, as A. E. himself has written:—

  "Away! the great life calls; I leave
    For Beauty, Beauty's rarest flower;
    For Truth, the lips that ne'er deceive;
    For Love, I leave Love's haunted bower."—

and these moments are but the influences toward
the exalted mood of the spirit. Of purely earthly
things he has written with great beauty; the soft,
veiled colors of Irish landscape are in his verses,
for A. E. is painter as well as poet, and, like other
painter poets, he has delighted to reproduce in his
verse somewhat of the glory that appeals to the
eye. He has written, too, of love, although of
love, not in its passion, but in the calm and the
quietude of soul that it engenders, and in the
spiritual desires which as spirit it arouses, but
which as a thing of earth it leaves unfulfilled:—

  "What is the love of shadowy lips
    That know not what they seek or press,
    From whom the lure for ever slips
    And fails their phantom tenderness?

"The mystery and light of eyes
  That near to mine grow dim and cold;
  They move afar in ancient skies
  Mid flame and mystic darkness rolled.

"O beauty, as thy heart o'erflows
  In tender yielding unto me,
  A vast desire awakes and grows
  Unto forgetfulness of thee."

In a degree, A. E.'s poetry is a reaction to the
philosophy of Catholicism, a protest against the
creed which decrees punishment for the soul that
has committed acts that it never promised not to
commit. He has voiced in certain poems the plea
which Frederick Ryan embodied in "Criticism
and Courage," for the freedom of intellect from
the dogma of religion. His belief in the cyclic
life of the soul—whether it be called theosophy or
Platonism matters little—involves also a belief
in the eternal freedom of the will:

"The power is ours to make or mar
  Our fate as on the earliest morn,
The Darkness and the Radiance are
  Creatures within the spirit born.
Yet, bathed in gloom too long, we might
Forget how we imagined light."

and this doctrine has accentuated the points of
difference between his creed and that of the greater
number of his countrymen. Conceiving, as he
does, that the soul of man is a part of the world-
spirit, it becomes impossible for him to postulate
a deity to whom the control of man's destiny is
intrusted; to him man is God in the degree that
his soul is in harmony with the spiritual life of the
world, and this harmony is attained more frequently in suffering than in joy. Thus, for him,
pain is not a punishment for sin, but the giver of
knowledge, the experience encountered by the
spirit in its quest for unity. To this belief he has
given expression in "The Man to the Angel":—

> "I have wept a million tears;
>   Pure and proud one, where are thine,
>   What the gain though all thy years
>   In unbroken beauty shine?
>
> "All your beauty can not win
>   Truth we learn in pain and sighs:
>   You can never enter in
>   To the circle of the wise.
>
> "They are but the slaves of light
>   Who have never known the gloom,
>   And between the dark and bright
>   Willed in freedom their own doom.

"Think not in your pureness there,
    That our pain but follows sin:
    There are fires for those who dare
    Seek the throne of might to win.

"Pure one, from your pride refrain:
    Dark and lost amid the strife
    I am myriad years of pain
    Nearer to the fount of life.

"When defiance fierce is thrown
    At the god to whom you bow,
    Rest the lips of the Unknown
    Tenderest upon my brow."

But it is less as a philosopher of protest that
A. E. will be remembered than as the poet of the
spirit, the Platonist, the believer in the dignity
of the soul of man, the worshipper of the spirit of
nature. He represents the national spirit of Ireland to a peculiar degree, for he is the singer of
that other world of which this is but the shadow,
that universe of the spirit that in Ireland, because
of her wrongs, has dominated the mind of men to
the exclusion of the material world of existence.
He represents above all her spirituality, her hope,
her aspiration, and the love of the beauty of her
landscape, and it is in him that Ireland has found
her fullest expression in modern poetry. And it

is in his noblest poem, "Reconciliation," that one may find the resolution of that mystic ecstasy of spirit in which the visionary attains unity with the Oversoul:—

"I begin through the grass once again to be bound to the Lord
  I can see, through a face that has faded, the face full of rest
  Of the earth, of the mother, my heart with her heart in accord,
  As I lie 'mid the cool green tresses that mantle her breast.
  I begin with the grass once again to be bound to the Lord.

"By the hand of a child I am led to the throne of the King
  For a touch that now fevers me not is forgotten and far,
  And His infinite sceptered hands that sway us can bring
  Me in dreams from the laugh of a child to the song of a star.
  On the laugh of a child I am borne to the joy of the King."

In that one of his essays in "Ideas of Good and Evil" (1903) entitled "What Is Popular Poetry?" William Butler Yeats has told us of the genesis

of his art.   It was in the activity of a "Young
Ireland" society, of which he had become a member, that his attention, and that of other young
men, was turned toward the ballad makers of
Ireland, and toward Ferguson, Allingham and
Davis and Mangan, and that he, together with
others who partook both of his political principles
and his literary taste, became ambitious that
Ireland should possess a national poetry of true
literary merit.   "I thought one day," he has
written, "if somebody could make a style which
would not be an English style and yet would be
musical and full of colour, many others would
catch fire from him, and we would have a really
great school of ballad poetry in Ireland.   If these
poets, who have never ceased to fill the newspapers
and the ballad-books, had a good tradition they
would write beautifully and move everybody as
they move me.   Then a little later on I thought
if they had something else to write about besides
political opinions, if more of them would write
about the beliefs of the people like Allingham, or
about old legends like Ferguson, they would find
it easier to get a style.   Then with a deliberate-
ness that still surprises me, for in my heart of
hearts I have never been quite certain that one

should be more than an artist, that even patriotism is more than an impure desire in an artist, I set to work to find a style and things to write about that the ballad writers might be the better.

"They are no better, I think, and my desire to make them so was, it may be, one of the illusions Nature holds before one, because she knows that the gifts she has to give are not worth troubling about. . . . She wanted a few verses from me, and because it would not have seemed worth while taking so much trouble to see my books lie on a few drawing room tables, she filled my head with thoughts of making a whole literature, and plucked me out of the Dublin art schools where I should have stayed drawing from the round, and sent me into a library to read bad translations from the Irish, and at last down into Connaught to sit by turf fires. I wanted to write 'popular poetry' like those Irish poets, for I believed that all good literatures were popular . . . and hated what I called the coteries. I thought that one must write without care, for that was of the coteries, but with a gusty energy that would put all straight if it came out of the right heart, . . .

"From that day to this I have been busy among the verses and stories that the people make for themselves, but I had been busy a very little while before I knew that what we call popular poetry never came from the people at all." And he goes on to say that true popular poetry relies upon a tradition of ideas and of speech, just as the poetry of "the coteries" relies upon a written tradition, and that both the written and the unwritten tradition play no part in that poetry which is "of the middle class," which contains no expression of idea or emotion that is not self-evident in the verse alone, and which is characterized by "that straightforward logic, as of newspaper articles, which so tickles the ears of the shopkeepers." This theory finds its logical complement in the views expressed in two earlier essays in the same volume, "The Symbolism of Poetry" and "Symbolism in Painting" in which the poet writes of his belief that poetry moves us because of its symbolism, and that symbols, created out of the tradition of centuries, emotional and intellectual, are the record of man's spiritual life, and afford him the sole refuge from the externality that we call experience, in that spiritual essence of which the soul lies dreaming.

Yeats's first volume, published in 1889 and containing, besides "The Wanderings of Oisin," a scene from his earliest play, "The Island of Statues" (1885), and a little play, "Mosada" (1886), and the first versions of some of the poems and ballads by which he is most likely to be remembered, showed no traces of the influences, literary and artistic, by which the character of his later work has been so largely determined. "The Wanderings of Oisin" is the first fruit of his reading in the libraries, a retelling of the old Irish legend of the colloquy between Oisin, the last of the Fianna, and St. Patrick. The legend runs that Oisin, the son of Finn, was sought by Neave, a beautiful maiden from the Land of the Ever Young, and rode with her over the sea until he came to her abiding place. There, beguiled by her beauty, he lived for three hundred years, which to him seemed as three, but often longed for the companionship of his fellow heroes. In order to appease him, Neave distracted him with many adventures, but these did not serve, and finally she set him upon the magic horse and sent him over the sea to Ireland, warning him that if he dismounted he would never be able to return to her. Arriving in Ireland, he found all changed. The men were miserable and weak, they sang no longer the joyous songs of old, and in the place of the raths of the king were the churches of a new and dismal religion. He learned that the Fianna had become merely a legend, that all had been dead for two centuries and more, and filled with sadness, he planned to return to Neave. On the shore some men, trying to move a sack of sand, fell, crushed by its weight, and Oisin, stooping from his horse, pitched the sack five yards with his hand. But the effort broke his saddle girth, he fell in the roadway, the horse disappeared, and bowed with the weight of three centuries he lost all hope. To him then comes St. Patrick, who has heard of his former prowess, and wishes to know of his "three centuries of dalliance with a demon thing." Oisin tells his story, and inquiring what has become of the Fianna, learns that they have been doomed to eternal damnation. Thereupon he recants his profession of Christianity, preferring to be with his comrades even in hell, to being in heaven among the weak who take no joy in life. The legend as Yeats has treated it breathes something of the same intellectual honesty, something of the same pagan view of the joylessness of Christianity that one finds in the tale of "Aucassin and Nicolette"; it has a certain philosophic value, quite apart from its poetic treatment, in the vigor with which it portrays the clash between the new ideals and the old. But the distinctive beauty of "The Wanderings of Oisin," as of all the work included in Yeats's earliest volume, is neither narrative nor dramatic, although he has given us examples of his manipulation of both of these methods of treatment, but lyrical. Patrick and Oisin represent less two opposing schools of thought than two different kinds of feeling about life, and hence two different values set upon it. It would be idle to say that the paganism of Oisin is less spiritual than the Christianity of Patrick, but it is perfectly true that their spirituality is that of emotion; neither reacts to life in terms of thought, but in their feeling. Oisin is in love with the visible beauty of life, with action, with the external, and with the familiar spirits that inhabit nature. To Patrick these things mean nothing, his interest lies in a life not of this world, to him the soul is of supreme importance, and his emotion finds its expression as naturally in asceticism as that of Oisin in exuberance. It is, however, in the suggestion of emotion through pictures of beauty in nature and of that imaginative beauty which he places in the land of faery, that Yeats excels in

this earliest volume, although in certain poems, of
which "King Goll" is the most notable example,
there is present that haunting beauty of a twilight
world which is his essential contribution to contemporary poetic feeling.

Yeats's career as a lyric poet practically closed
in 1899 when he began to devote his entire attention to writing for the theater, the interest always
nearest his heart. He had by then already
written, besides the two plays of his youth since
withdrawn, "Mosada" (1886) and "The Island
of Statues" (1885); "The Countess Cathleen"
(1892–97) and "The Land of Heart's Desire"
(1894). Since 1899 he has published but one
volume of verse, "The Wind Among the Reeds"
(1902), and the few songs interspersed in his plays.
It is interesting to note that in 1902 he determined
to write all of his long poems for the theater, and
his short ones for the psaltery, an instrument which
was constructed for him by Arnold Dolmetsch,
who became interested in Yeats's experiments at
the Abbey in the rendering of dramatic poetry.
But this resolution did not change the essential
character of his poetry, and although his theories
of dramatic and lyric expression have undoubtedly
influenced the interpretation of his plays by the

Abbey company, the diction which he invented,
and which was first employed by Miss Florence
Farr, is no longer used even in the presentation of
his own plays.

There are two dominant motives in his lyric
poetry, love of woman and the cult of the mystic;
and to these must be added, although in a lesser
degree, the love of external nature which influenced
the composition of "The Lake Isle of Innisfree,"
and which he has since repudiated. In both of
these themes he has excelled, and in his treatment of both he has made a distinct and unique
contribution to the poetry of English literature.

In order to understand in just what this contribution consists, it will be necessary to refer to
the philosophy upon which his poetry is founded,
and of which he has written in explanation in
several essays. It is important to note, however,
that for the most part these essays were written
after the turning point in his poetic career, in 1899,
and that although he had been both an editor and a
critic of modern Irish literature in the years immediately preceding, the formulation of his philosophy and of his esthetics in criticism was not
accomplished until after he had turned from lyric
poetry to the drama. At first sight, it might be

said that Yeats, like Coleridge, became a philosopher and a critic only when his poetic inspiration was at its lowest ebb, were it not for the fact that his interest in the philosophy of magic and the psychology of mysticism can be dated as early as 1886, when he was a member of the Hermetic Society, of which A. E. was, and still is, the leader. It is difficult, therefore, to account for the change in the character of his poetry, to explain just what was the influence that turned his verse from the path of explicit and melodious lyricism into one of subtle intention clothed in obscure symbols. On the basis of internal evidence the task is impossible; all that can be said is that such a change did take place about 1895, and that the poet himself has supplied, in his essays, some commentary on his work. For the purpose of making clear the attitude of his later work, three passages may be quoted from his essays; the first from "Symbolism in Painting," the second from "Symbolism in Poetry" and the third from "Magic."

"All art that is not mere story-telling, or mere portraiture, is symbolic, and has the purpose of those symbolic talismans which medieval magicians made with complex colours and forms, and bade their patients ponder over daily, and guard with holy secrecy; for it entangles, in complex colours and forms, a part of the Divine Essence. A person or a landscape that is a part of a story or a portrait, evokes but so much emotion as the story or the portrait can permit without loosening the bonds that make it a story or a portrait; but if you liberate a person or a landscape from the bonds of motives and their actions, causes and their effects, and from all bonds but the bonds of your love, it will change under your eyes, and become a symbol of an infinite emotion, a perfected emotion, a part of the Divine Essence; for we love nothing but the perfect, and our dreams make all things perfect, that we may love them. Religious and visionary people, monks and nuns, medicine-men and opium-eaters, see symbols in their trances; for religious and visionary thought is thought about perfection and the way to perfection; and symbols are the only things free enough from all bonds to speak of perfection."

"If people were to accept the theory that poetry moves us because of its symbolism, what change should one look for in the manner of our poetry? A return to the way of our fathers, a casting out of descriptions of nature for the sake of nature, of the moral law for the sake of the moral law, a

casting out of all anecdotes and of that brooding
over scientific opinion that so often distinguished
the central flame in Tennyson, and of that vehe-
mence that would make us do or not do certain
things; or, in other words, we should come to
understand that the beryl stone was enchanted
by our fathers that it might unfold the pictures
in its heart, and not to mirror our own excited
faces, or the boughs waving outside the window.
With this change of substance, this return to
imagination, this understanding that the laws of
art, which are the hidden laws of the world, can
alone bind the imagination, would come a change
of style, and we would cast out of serious poetry
those energetic rhythms, as of a man running,
which are the invention of the will with its eyes
always on something to be done or undone; and
we would seek out those wavering, meditative,
organic rhythms, which are the embodiment of
the imagination, that neither desires nor hates,
because it has done with time, and only wishes to
gaze upon some reality, some beauty; nor would it
be any longer possible for anybody to deny the importance of form, in all its kinds, for although you
can expound an opinion or describe a thing when
your words are not quite well chosen, you cannot

give a body to something that moves beyond the senses, unless your words are as subtle, as complex, as full of mysterious life as the body of a flower or of a woman. The form of sincere poetry, unlike the form of popular poetry, may indeed be sometimes obscure or ungrammatical as in some of the best of the Songs of Innocence and Experience, but it must have the perfections that escape analysis, the subtleties that have a new meaning every day, and it must have all this whether it be but a little song made out of a moment of dreamy indolence, or some great epic made out of the dreams of one poet and of a hundred generations whose hands were never weary of the sword."

"I believe in the practice and philosophy of what we have agreed to call magic, in what I must call the evocation of spirits though I do not know what they are, in the power of creating magical illusions, in the visions of truth in the depths of the mind when the eyes are closed; and I believe in three doctrines, which have, as I think, been handed down from early times, and been the foundations of nearly all magical practices. These doctrines are—

"(1) That the borders of our mind are ever shifting, and that many minds can flow into one another, as it were, and create or reveal a single mind, a single energy.

" (2) That the borders of our memories are as shifting, and that our memories are a part of one great memory, the memory of Nature herself.

" (3) That this great mind and great memory can be evoked by symbols."

In these three quotations are summed up the cardinal points of his philosophy and of his esthetics; and they serve to explain the deliberate intention underlying much of his poetry. But in no sense is Yeats's poetry expressive of a positive philosophy of life, and this for two reasons. His view of life is purely negative, and does not partake of the affirmation of life that is found in the poetry of another mystic, A. E.; and the philosophy of his art is founded upon an explicit denial of Arnold's theory that poetry is "a criticism of life." Indeed, for him, the function of poetry is to produce in the hearer, through the rhythm of the verse, a psychological condition bordering upon trance, and then evoke "the great mind and great memory" through symbols. In other words, the purpose of his poetry is to play upon those moods and emotions that have no place in the waking life of energy and activity. And in this theory lies the core of both his theory of art, and his philosophy of life. He has expressed this view of life in some very beautiful lines in "The Shadowy Waters" (1900), which since they condition the fundamental attitude of all his poetry, may well be quoted here.

> "All would be well
> Could we but give us wholly to the dreams,
> And get into their world that to the sense
> Is shadow, and not linger wretchedly
> Among substantial things; for it is dreams
> That lift us to the flowing, changing world
> That the heart longs for. What is love itself,
> Even though it be the lightest of light love,
> But dreams that hurry from beyond the world
> To make low laughter more than meat and drink,
> Though it but set us sighing? Fellow-wanderer,
> Could we but mix ourselves into a dream,
> Not in its image on the mirror!"

I have said that Yeats's unique contribution to poetic feeling lies in this dream-like, haunting, other-world spirit that his poetry evokes, and that this has been expressed most characteristically in the poems dealing with love and with mysticism. The essential quality of his love-poetry is that it deals with love not as the passionate and compelling emotion that we know it to be in actual life, but in the terms of a life totally different than the experience of actuality, an existence that is wholly disembodied, a life purely of the spirit, and of a spirit that feels but faintly, vaguely, and with a passion in which sex plays no part. Crashaw, the first English mystic poet of importance, wrote of religious ecstasy in the terms of earthly love; the Preraphaelites, who were symbolists, dealt with love as a thing of sense, in symbols and ideals that have their foundation in purely physical beauty, but Yeats is the first English poet who has treated of earthly love as a thing wholly of the spirit, existing only in a dream of mystic ecstasy, in which physical beauty is totally immaterial excepting as the visible clothing of the soul itself. This is the distinguishing quality of such a poem as "The Rose of the World":—

"Who dreamed that beauty passes like a dream?
      For these red lips for all their mournful pride,
      Mournful that no new wonder may betide,
Troy passes away in one high funeral gleam,
      And Usna's children died.

"We and the labouring world are passing by:
      Amid men's souls, that waver and give place,
      Like the pale waters in their wintry race,

Under the passing stars, foam of the sky,
　　Lives on this lonely face.

" Bow down, archangels, in your dim abode:
　　Before you were, or any hearts to beat,
　　Weary and kind one lingered by His seat;
　He made the world to be a grassy road
　　Before her wandering feet."

or of these lines:—

"Fasten your hair with a golden pin,
　And bind up every wandering tress;
　I bade my heart build these poor rhymes:
　It worked at them, day out, day in,
　Building a sorrowful loveliness
　Out of the battles of old times.

" You need but lift a pearl-pale hand,
　And bind up your long hair and sigh;
　And all men's hearts must burn and beat;
　And candle-like foam on the dim sand,
　And stars climbing the dew-dropping sky,
　Live but to light your passing feet."

and of these, in which "He Tells of the Perfect
Beauty":—

"O cloud-pale eyelids, dream-dimmed eyes,
　The poets labouring all their days
　To build a perfect beauty in rhyme
　Are overthrown by a woman's gaze

And by the unlabouring brood of the skies:
And therefore my heart will bow, when dew
Is dropping sleep, until God burn time,
Before the unlabouring stars and you."

Of the poems of mysticism, three of the most
famous may be quoted, since they too express
Yeats's disbelief in the life of actuality, and his
conviction that the life of dream is the life of
reality:—

"Time drops in decay,
  Like a candle burnt out,
  And the mountains and woods
  Have their day, have their day;
  What one in the rout
  Of the fire-born moods
  Has fallen away?"

"O sweet everlasting Voices, be still;
  Go to the guards of the heavenly fold
  And bid them wander obeying your will
  Flame under flame, till Time be no more;
  Have you not heard that our hearts are old,
  That you call in birds, in wind on the hill,
  In shaken boughs, in tide on the shore?
  O sweet everlasting Voices, be still."

"Out-worn heart, in a time out-worn,
  Come clear of the nets of wrong and right;
  Laugh, heart, again in the grey twilight,
  Sigh, heart, again in the dew of the morn.

"Your mother Eire is always young,
  Dew ever shining and twilight grey;
  Though hope fall from you and love decay,
  Burning in fires of a slanderous tongue.

"Come, heart, where hill is heaped upon hill:
  For there the mystical brotherhood
  Of sun and moon and hollow and wood
  And river and stream work out their will;

"And God stand winding his lonely horn,
  And time and the world are ever in flight;
  And love is less kind than the grey twilight,
  And hope is less dear than the dew of the morn."

It seems impossible not to believe that these
poems and others like them, made, as was the
case with "Cap and Bells," out of a world of
dreams, do not contain Yeats's most characteristically personal expression. It may be well
asked, however, what has become of the Yeats
who wrote:—

> "Know, that I would accounted be
>   True brother of that company,
>   Who sang to sweeten Ireland's wrong,
>   Ballad and story, rann and song."

and the answer is not, at first sight, quite evident.
But there is another phase of Yeats's work, espe-

cially evident in such plays as "The Countess
Cathleen" (1892–97), and "Cathleen ni Houlihan" (1902); in that beautiful collection of folk-
lore, "The Celtic Twilight" (1893), and in "Stories
of Red Hanrahan" (1904); in poems like "The
Ballad of Moll Magee," "The Ballad of Father
O'Hart," "Down by the Salley Gardens" and
"The Withering of the Boughs" in which the
essence of Ireland is manifest. He himself has
written, in an essay upon "The Celtic Element in
Literature," that the Celtic movement has meant
for him only the unsealing of the fountain of
Celtic tradition, and the discovery and employment of its beautiful legend and folk-lore. It
is by busying himself with this fund of folk-lore
and tradition that he has come to feel and to express Ireland; not, indeed, the Ireland of Synge
or of Lady Gregory, nor that of the younger school
of playwrights, nor that of Doctor Hyde, but the
Ireland of the imagination. Zola's definition of
art as nature seen through a temperament is peculiarly germane to the interpretation of Yeats.
And although during certain periods of his development as a poet temperament has, in the final
analysis, crowded out nature from his verse, that
part of his poetry which is likely to prove most

enduring expresses not only the spiritual qualities
of the imaginative and emotionally sensitive Irish
peasant, but the beautiful landscape of the western
counties, Mayo, Sligo, Galway, the natural beauty
of which has been accentuated by association with
the noble legends of the past.

Just what, it may be asked, is the nature of the
literary experience that awaits the reader of
Yeats's poetry? The total effect of his verse is
emotional; it is less the poetry of a man who, like
Lucretius, or Milton, or Wordsworth, or Tennyson,
has been stirred profoundly by ideas, for whom the
impelling necessity for expression was the result
of an emotional reaction to intellectual conflict,
than that of a spiritually and emotionally sensitive
personality, keenly aware of beauty, whose imagination has been quickened by the nobility and the
poetry of the past, a man who has little in common with the temper of contemporary life. His
attitude toward life is founded upon an emotional
philosophy, upon feeling deeply about life rather
than thinking deeply about it, upon truth revealed
in a moment of spiritual dilation rather than upon
truth apprehended and made by the intelligent
exercise of the reason. In other words, the fundamental attitude of his poetry is that of the

mystic as opposed to that of the scientist; indeed
Yeats, coming as he did after Tennyson and after
the widespread interest in science that preoccupied the later Victorians, may be considered as
part of the reactionary movement that was influenced by the Preraphaelites, which, disbeliev-
ing both in modern science and in modern life,
turned toward its emotions rather than to its intelligence for an interpretation and a solution of
life, and sought art as a refuge.   Yeats has been
influenced in his feelings about life by Jacob
Boehme and the Rosicrucians, and, particularly,
by William Blake; less perhaps by the Blake of
the "Songs of Innocence and Experience" than
by the Blake of "Jerusalem" and the "Prophetic
Books."   It must be remembered, however, that
Yeats is not a philosophic poet in the sense that
A. E. is a philosophic poet; the philosophic aspect
of his poetry lies in its form rather than in its
content; like John Lylly, John Donne and Walter
Pater, he has a philosophy of style, but his view
of life is most clearly stated not in his poetry, but
in his essays.   He is preeminently the poet's poet
of our time, for his inspiration has come less from
life than from literature, and his art has been influenced and moulded by the contemplation of

beautiful things, until, from a poet who desired to express an immediate reaction to life, he developed into the poet of our time whose verse has had the least connection with contemporary activity, and whose especial contribution has been, to borrow a phrase from A. E., to reveal to us "the spirit as the weaver of beauty."

William Sharp, who from 1893 until his death in 1905 contributed to the literature of the Celtic renascence in prose and in verse over the pseudonym of "Fiona MacLeod," was influenced by the poetry of A. E. and of Yeats. He was not an Irishman, having been born in 1855 in the west highlands of Scotland; as a young man he went to London, and there came under the influence of D. G. Rossetti, who became his friend and literary adviser. He experimented with poetry, but achieved his reputation as a critic and editor, and later as a writer of fiction. In 1886 he suffered a severe illness, during which a world of dream and of vision was opened to him, and upon his recovery he interested himself in psychic research. In 1893 Fiona Macleod published "Pharais," the first of a long series of prose romances the author of which was given out to be a cousin of Mrs. Sharp's for whom Sharp acted as sponsor. Be-

POETRY OF THE RENASCENCE   61

cause of the mystery surrounding "her," because
of Sharp's known fondness for mystification—he
had once edited and written a whole review under
eight pseudonyms—, and because of certain de-
ductions made from the comparison of the work
of Fiona MacLeod and of William Sharp, many
critics suspected them of being one and the same
person. The acknowledgment of their identity
was, however, made public only in 1912 by the
authoritative publication of his diaries and letters
in a memoir by his wife. These show that Sharp
believed himself possessed of a dual existence; a
vivid emotional existence that he personified as
Fiona MacLeod, and his crowded life as novelist
and critic, dependent upon his writing for his
livelihood, the life of William Sharp. The distinction seems to rest upon the dominance of one
mood over the other; the emotional mood was
that of Fiona, the intellectual, that of Sharp.   In
so far as it affects his verse, the psychological
problem is almost negligible, for the sole advantage
of his pseudonym was that it enabled him to
write, as he believed, from the point of view of a
woman, in such poems as those included in "From
the Heart of a Woman," and, in certain other
poems, to indulge without fear of censure in an

ecstatic emotionalism of which, as the keenly intellectual critic, he may have been suspicious.

His interest as a poet was given almost wholly
to the exploration of the spiritual world revealed
in dreams, and to the body of legendary lore
common to Ireland and Scotland; with such interests it is not surprising that the chief influences
upon his poetic expression were those of A. E. and
of William Butler Yeats. In "The Dirge of the
Four Cities" he writes like Yeats, and in "Dim
Face of Beauty" the agreement with A. E. is
quite apparent. But although he was largely
imitative, he wrote not a few poems of distinction
in which he attained an utterance of his own, and
it is surprising to find this utterance so completely
different from the heavily laden form of his prose.
He is at his best in little poems such as "The
Vision":—

> "In a fair place
>   Of whin and grass,
>   I heard feet pass
>   Where no one was.
>
> "I saw a face
>   Bloom like a flower—
>   Nay, as the rainbow shower
>   Of a tempestuous hour.

"It was not man, nor woman:
   It was not human:
   But, beautiful and wild
   Terribly undefiled,
   I knew an unborn child."

or "Day and Night":—

"From grey to dusk, the veils unfold
   To pearl and amethyst and gold—
      Thus is the new day woven and spun:

"From glory of blue to rainbow-spray
   From sunset-gold to violet-grey—
      Thus is the restful night re-won."

which, in spite of their almost lapidary simplicity of expression, interpret a mood with singular beauty and fullness. These little poems express their suggestion almost always through the use of pictures, but even more important than this idyllic quality is the striking sense of word color and word harmony that Sharp must have possessed in order to have written them. In the inevitability of their phrasing, in their unity of form and content, in their delicate interpretation of a mood through the color and the music of words, they stand in the front rank of minor poetry. And all the poetry that Sharp put forth under the name of Fiona MacLeod is essentially that of a spirit sensitive to the fainter shadings of emotion, at its best the revelation of subjective nuances.

In dealing with Lionel Johnson we come to a poet the best of whose work equals in value anything that English poets have produced during the last twenty-five years. If, as is unfortunately the case, he must be classed among the minor poets, it is rather because the quantity of his best work is very small than because it is deficient in quality. His poetry reflects the deep and abiding love in which he held the four chief influences in his spiritual and intellectual life: Winchester, his school, the languages and literatures of Greece and Rome, Ireland, and the religion of the Church of Rome. His life was brief, and tragic in its incompleteness. He died in 1902.

He was not, like A. E., a philosophic poet, nor like Yeats, an innovator in spirit, a weaver of strange harmonies in beautiful language. His progenitor in the verse of Ireland was Aubrey de Vere, between whose stately, meditative poems and the work of Lionel Johnson there are many points of contact. He belongs rather with Francis Thompson and with Mrs. Meynell, to the little group of meditative poets of Catholicism that flourished during the last two decades of the past

century, than to the circle of so-called decadents
with which he was connected by the ties of friend-
ship. Unlike Dowson and Symons, and the other
poets of the nineties, Johnson was not a romanticist; the influence of Pater and of Wilde is not
felt in his verse, he did not seek to express the
sordid phases of physical or of emotional life, he
did not believe, as did Yeats, in the tenets of the
"esthetic movement." He was in every sense
of the word a classicist, a faultless technician in
the accepted forms, a writer of poetry that fulfilled the requirement set for it by Milton—that
it be simple, sensuous and passionate. He was a
religious mystic, and his philosophy of life was
tinged with pantheism, a quality that is rarely
absent from the poetry of those of an innately
religious disposition who care very greatly for
nature. In his devotion to the cause of nationalism in Ireland and to the Catholic religion, he
found himself in somewhat the same position as
that of the cavalier poets of the seventeenth century, and in a poem entitled "Mystic and Cavalier" he set forth his reaction to the life of his
time:—

"Go from me: I am one of those, who fall.
What! hath no cold wind swept your heart at all,

In my sad company? Before the end,
   Go from me, dear my friend!

"Yours are the victories of light: your feet
  Rest from good toil, where rest is brave and sweet,
  But after warfare in a mourning gloom,
    I rest in clouds of doom.

"Have you not read so, looking in these eyes?
  Is it the common light of the pure skies,
  Lights up their shadowy depths? The end is set:
    Though the end be not yet.

"When gracious music stirs, and all is bright,
  And beauty triumphs through a courtly night;
  When I too joy, a man like other men:
    Yet, am I like them, then?

"And in the battle, when the horsemen sweep
  Against a thousand deaths, and fall on sleep:
  Who ever sought that sudden calm, if I
    Sought not? Yet, could not die.

"Seek with thine eyes to pierce this crystal sphere:
  Canst read a fate there, prosperous and clear?
  Only the mists, only the weeping clouds:
    Dimness, and airy shrouds.

"Beneath, what angels are at work? What powers
  Prepare the secret of the fatal hours?
  See! the mists tremble, and the clouds are stirred:
    When comes the calling word?

"The clouds are breaking from the crystal ball,
    Breaking and clearing: and I look to fall.
When the cold winds and airs of portent sweep,
        My spirit may have sleep.

"O rich and sounding voices of the air!
    Interpreters and prophets of despair:
    Priests of a fearful sacrament! I come
        To make with you mine home."

In several singularly noble poems, the most famous
of which is "Ways of War," dedicated to the Irish
patriot, John O'Leary, he recorded a passionate
love for Ireland, and his belief that her glorious
destiny among the nations would work itself out
once more in battle. And his classical learning
was such that he was able to write many of his
most beautiful religious poems in Latin.

The chief effect of his poetry upon the reader
is a sense of the power of his deep reflective mood,
a sense of the scholarly and cherishing care of his
expression, a feeling that he, like the poets of the
seventeenth century from whom he learned his
technique, was a master of melody and rhythm
and cadence. Two little poems, although they
do not deal with any of his four loves, bring this
to the reader's attention with characteristic vivid-
ness, and to this end may be quoted. They are

entitled "Harmonies," are dedicated to Vincent
O'Sullivan, and were written in 1889.

I

"Sweet music lingers
From her harpstrings on her fingers,
When they rest in mine:
And her clear glances
Help the music, whereto dances,
Trembling with an hope divine,
Every heart: and chiefly mine.

"Could she discover
All her heart to any lover,
She who sways them all?
Yet her hand trembles,
Laid in mine: and scarce dissembles,
That its music looks to fall
Into mine, and Love end all."

II

"The airs, that best belong,
Upon the strings devoutly playing,
Your heart devoutly praying:
Now sound your passion, full and strong,
Past all her fond gainsaying.

"First, strangely sweet and low,
Slowly her careless ears entrancing:
Then set the music dancing,
And wild notes flying to and fro;
Like spirited sunbeams glancing.

"The melodies will stir
Spirits of love, that still attend her:
That able are to bend her,
By subtile arts transforming her;
And all their wisdom lend her.

"Last, loud and resolute,
Ring out a triumph and a greeting!
No call for sad entreating,
For she will grant you all your suit,
Her song your music meeting."

Of Johnson's generation and period, and, like
him, influenced in her art by a devout belief in
Catholicism, Mrs. Katherine Tynan Hinkson has
written not a few excellent poems, and some
stories of country life and character. Her range
in poetry is more limited than that of Johnson,
her mood is not as austere, not as deeply reflective,
and she has been influenced less by the mystic
aspect of her religion. She has chosen to express
the religious ideals that found embodiment in the
life and in the teaching of Saint Francis of Assisi,
and the chief characteristics of her poetic feeling
are a certain delicate sympathy with the weak,
the helpless, with children and with animals, and
an instinctive love for the beautiful in nature. Of
these things she has sung with charm, and often

with great beauty, but her verse has never achieved the distinguishing flame of Johnson's, the ecstasy of A. E.'s, the exquisite harmony or the haunting beauty of Yeats's.

Of far greater importance, both as an influence upon the later writers of the renascence, and because of the unusual quality of his own poetic gifts, are the two volumes of poetry that Doctor Douglas Hyde has published: "Love Songs of Connacht" (1894) and "Religious Songs of Connacht" (1906). They are compilations of the folk-songs of a single province, carefully noted down, edited and translated by Doctor Hyde. The original poems have become part of the Gaelic literature that has been growing up in Ireland, but the influence of Doctor Hyde's beautiful translations can hardly be overestimated. He for the first time employed in literature the peasant dialect which has since become a recognized medium of artistic expression, later to be employed by one of the greatest dramatists of modern times, John Millington Synge. The chief characteristic of Doctor Hyde's prose translations of Gaelic poetry is their concreteness of expression; the use of Anglo-Irish has contributed to modern English letters not so much a new vocabulary as a way of looking at life that, coming in a period of academic detachment, excites in the reader the superb shock of the unexpectedly inevitable. This diction, picturesque, romantic, and, as some of us feel, highly imaginative, cannot be acquired through a careful choice in vocabulary; it depends upon an immediate reaction to life in expression, a reaction that, to a certain extent, is wholly unconscious of any art. It depends, also, upon an accuracy of observation and a truth in the registering of emotions that is as unconscious of its effect as that of a child. It is rather the result of unsophisticated observation, untutored in what convention demands that it shall see, of the immediate and vigorous expression of whatever experience it has come in contact with, than of anything as artificial as a "style." It is the language of emotional excitement, uncontrolled by convention, unsophisticated in its observation of experience, immediate in its expression, and like all highly imaginative diction, it has its fundamental basis in the accurate vision of reality. The frequent inversion of word order, the elision of words, and numerous other characteristics which are apt to affect the reader as being mere tricks of style lose their apparent artificiality when it is remembered

that Anglo-Irish, as it is actually spoken in the
west, is nothing other than a literal translation of
idiomatic Gaelic into English, preserving in the
transition the grammar, the word order, and the
diction of Gaelic. Indeed, Anglo-Irish as a medium of literary expression is little more than the
substitution of English words for the original
Gaelic.

The influence of Doctor Hyde's work is very
evident in the later poetry of Alfred Percival
Graves who, having been born in 1846, may justly
be regarded as the dean of modern Irish letters,
and who will always be remembered among Irishmen as the author of the rollicking ballad of
"Father O'Flynn." His earlier work is chiefly
lyrical and, like Thomas Moore, he claims old
Irish melodies as the source of his inspiration.
The distinguishing quality of his lyrics is their
abundant humor; this and their singing rhythms
justify the comparison between Graves and Samuel Lover made by Doctor Hyde, and indicate a
further comparison between much of his work and
a certain mood to be found in the poetry of Burns.
These songs are chiefly of the Irish countryside,
of its life, of its characters, of its aspirations;
written before Doctor Hyde published his transla-

tions in Anglo-Irish, their expression is that of an Englishman recording the peculiarities of speech among the Irish. In his later work, "Songs of the Gael" (1908) and "A Gaelic Story Telling" (1908), he has preserved both his humor and his lyrical gifts intact, but, as Doctor Hyde himself had noted, the Irish renascence has produced both a change of feeling and a change in the medium of expression employed. Many of these poems are translations into the original Irish meter from the prose of Kuno Meyer, others do not show as directly the influence of the rediscovery of old Celtic legends, but implicit in all of Graves's later work is a certain seriousness of attitude toward Ireland that is not to be found in his earlier poems.

The work of another pioneer in the translation of folk-song, Doctor George Sigerson, is of great importance in having indicated the direction to be taken in preserving this body of popular art. His labors have extended over a period of forty years, but his most recent volume, "The Saga of King Lir," published as lately as 1913, betrays no diminution of his poetic gifts. He was among the first to retell the old legends in beautiful and stately verse and noble prose. His "Bards of the

Gael and Gall" (1897) is a treasure house for the lover of Ireland's folk-lore. In this he has been followed by T. W. Rolleston, critic, poet and editor, who has contributed widely to scholarship and to literature in his versions of the old legends. "Deirdre" (1897), "Myths and Legends of the Celtic Race" (1911), and "Sea Spray" (1909), evidence not only his scholarly attitude toward the content of his art; but also the distinction of his expression in both poetry and prose. Americans will remember him gratefully as the first translator into German of Whitman's "Leaves of Grass."

Among the feminine poets of the renascence there are not a few with as sure a claim to notability of accomplishment as that of Mrs. Hinkson. "Ethna Carberry" (Mrs. Seumas Mac-Manus) has written, in "The Four Winds of Erin" (1901), out of the heart of the sorrows and the dreams of Ireland in many poems, the best known of which is "The Passing of the Gael." "Moira O'Neill" (Mrs. Nesta Higginson Skrine) has written powerfully of her love of the countryside and of the Irish landscape, in "Songs of the Glens of Antrim" (1901), while Mrs. Nora Hopper Chesson has revealed herself a master of poetic expression and has clothed eternal emotions in the symbols of a legendary past. Dora Sigerson Shorter (Mrs. Clement Shorter) has become known chiefly as a balladist; her "Collected Poems" (1907), earned the high praise of no less discerning a critic than George Meredith. In the lyric form her ability to convey reality, to render a mood in a few deft lines, and her chief excellences, compression, restraint and dramatic power are no less apparent, and readers will find her "New Poems" (1913) and "Madge Linsey and Other Poems" (1913), equally distinguished.

In 1904 A. E. edited a little volume of poems entitled "New Songs," comprising a selection from the poetry of eight of the then young craftsmen and craftswomen in verse to whom he had been both teacher and guide. All eight have since become well known to lovers of poetry in Ireland, and have thus fulfilled his prediction of their fame. Alice Milligan has written many patriotic poems of noteworthy excellence, and not a few having as their subjects episodes famous in the legendary history of Ireland. Her best known work is comprised in "Hero Lays" (1908). Eva Gore-Booth, Susan Mitchell and Ella Young have all been influenced by the tendency toward a mystic interpretation of life that has found its most enduring expression in the poetry of A. E. himself. Miss Gore-Booth's volume of verse, "The Egyptian Pillar" (1908), is remarkable for its lyric cadence, while the "Poems" (1908), of Miss Young possess a beauty of phrasing that is distinctly individual, and give expression to an almost religious ecstasy. Miss Mitchell, who is the secretary of the I. A. O. S. and one of the founders of the United Irishwomen, has written in "The Living Chalice" (1913), some rarely beautiful poems, finely sustained in their high idealism, and in expression marked by a superb frankness of imagery and symbol. In a little volume called "Aide to the Immortality of Certain Persons in Ireland" (1913), she has satirized with great humor many of the well known figures of the Celtic renascence.

Among the men whose work is represented in "New Songs" are Padraic Colum, Seumas O'Sullivan, Thomas Keohler and George Roberts. To these names must be added those of Joseph Campbell, Herbert Trench, Charles Weekes, James Stephens, John Millington Synge, Patrick MacGill, Thomas MacDonagh, Seumas MacManus, Norreys Jephson O'Connor, and, latest of all, Francis Ledwidge.

Padraic Colum is, although undeservedly, more widely known as a dramatist than as a poet. The single volume of his verse, "Wild Earth," was published in 1907 and contains but twenty-five poems. In his work and in that of Francis Ledwidge are sounded the two most distinctively original notes in the poetry of the younger generation of Irish writers. He is concerned both as poet and as dramatist with elemental emotions only; the subtle, the complex and the intricate in thought and in feeling do not enter into the scope of his work. Professor Weygandt [1] has pointed out that his chief themes are three in number: love of land, of woman, and of adventure. In his poems, for all their hardness and objectivity, for all their revolt against the bequeathed convention that involves an eternal acceptance of hardship, of squalor, physical and spiritual, of despair, the dominant note is one of courage to assume the adventure of life and of joy in its beauty. His best known single poem is "The Plougher," which, since it comprises the essence of his reaction to the life of his country, may well be quoted:—

"Sunset and silence! A man: around him earth savage, earth broken;
Beside him two horses—a plough!

[1] "Irish Plays and Playwrights," Houghton-Mifflin, 1913, pp. 199.

"Earth savage, earth broken, the dawn-man there in
the sunset,
And the Plough that is twin to the Sword, that is
founder of cities!

"Brute-tamer, plough-maker, earth breaker!
Can'st hear? There are ages between us.
Is it praying you are as you stand there
alone in the sunset?

"Surely your thoughts are of Pan, or of Wotan, or
of Dana?

"Yet why give thought to the gods? Has Pan led you
brutes where they stumble?
Has Dana numbed pain of the child-bed, or Wotan
put hands to your plough?

"What matter your foolish reply! O, man, standing
lone and bowed earthward,
Your task is a day near its close. Give thanks to
the night-giving God.

"Slowly the darkness falls, the broken lands blend
with the savage;
The brute-tamer stands by the brutes, a head's
breadth only above them.

"A head's breadth? Ay, but therein is hell's depth,
and the height up to heaven,
And the thrones of the gods and their halls, their
chariots, purples and splendours."

Padraic Colum is just as surely the poet of the future as Yeats is the poet of the past, and Stephens the poet of the present in Ireland.

Seumas O'Sullivan, Thomas Keohler and George Roberts, together with Charles Weekes, are followers of the mystic tradition. O'Sullivan's earliest volume, "The Twilight People" (1904), brought him forward as a master of delicate and faint rhythms, and a visionary whose poetry evoked in the minds of those to whom it was attuned memories and dreams of a spiritual life different from that of this world. He followed it with "Verses Sacred and Profane" (1908), "The Earth Lover" (1909), "Selected Lyrics" (1910). In the same year his "Collected Poems" were published, and in 1914, "An Epilogue." He has unswervingly preserved the fine qualities of his earlier work, and, although he has concerned himself neither with the past nor the present of his country, he has expressed its mystic idealism with exquisite and fragile beauty.

Thomas Keohler in "Songs of a Devotee" (1906), and George Roberts in "White Fire" (1908), have added to the store of lyrics expressive of the mystic interpretation of life of which the renascence has been productive. Charles Weekes

in "About Women" (1907), has written satirically
and quite without the vein of mysticism that runs
through his earlier poetry. Herbert Trench, before deserting the Irish movement for the management of a London theater, wrote in "Deirdre
Wed and Nineteen Other Poems" (1901), some
very beautiful verse dealing principally with heroic
legend. Joseph Campbell in known as an artist,
dramatist and poet. His volume of verse, "A
Mountainy Singer" (1909), and a volume of
prose impressions, "Mearing Stones" (1911), are
instinct with the life of Donegal.

The "Poems and Translations" (1909), of John
Millington Synge were, for the most part, written
between 1891 and 1908. They express the reaction against the tenuous mysticism and complex
imagery of Yeats and of A. E. that is to be likewise found in his plays. Their chief value is not
that of pure poetic content, but that of personal
expression; they reveal, even more clearly than
his plays, the temperament and the attitude
toward life of their author. "The strong things
of life," he wrote in the preface, "are needed in
poetry also, to show that what is exalted or tender
is not made by feeble blood. It may almost be
said that before verse can be human again it must

learn to be brutal." In his revolt against the otherworldliness of Irish poetry, Synge went to the other extreme, and the greater part of his verse is violent and truculent in its relation to life. He wrote sardonically and bitterly of his own life, and with Elizabethan frankness of the lives of others, but of nature he wrote tenderly and with beauty of vision. His translations are almost unmatched for the fidelity of their feeling to that of the original. But, in the final analysis, his accomplishment was less in poetry than in the drama, and it can be discussed to greater advantage in its relation to his dramatic writing.

The reaction instituted by the plays of Synge has been carried further in the poetry of Patrick MacGill and of James Stephens. Patrick Mac-Gill has written of his early experiences in two novels of stark realism, "Children of the Dead End" (1914), and "The Rat Pit" (1915). He came of an impoverished family in Donegal, labored on the farms, and later became one of the many casual and migratory laborers who cross each summer from Ireland to Scotland to help gather in the crops. Of the horrors of this life the uninitiated may read in his novels. "Songs of the Dead End" (1912), reveal both beauty and tragedy and are instinct with a philosophy that is a product of experience alone.

James Stephens has done his most important work as a novelist, although he commenced his literary career with a volume of verse, "Insurrections" (1909), and followed it with "The Hill of Vision" (1912), "Songs From the Clay" (1915) and "The Rocky Road to Dublin" (1916). His poetry is, for the most part, powerful and grim with the facts of life, from which he seeks no refuge in a world of heroic legend or ideality. He is not insensible to beauty, but humanity, as A. E. has pointed out in a charming essay, is Stephens' fundamental concern. He is in full rebellion against the school that upholds art as an alternative to life, saturating its work with dream and illusion. He is a satirist, a castigator of society, a realist of indubitable power.

Thomas MacDonagh, critic, dramatist, and leader in the ill-fated insurrection of April, 1916, was the author of three volumes of verse: "Through the Ivory Gate," "The Golden Joy," and "Songs of Myself" (1910). In his poetry he fused a highly mystical love of beauty with a passionate devotion to the national ideal and the rich destiny which he conceived as the future of

the Irish race. He expressed, perhaps unconsciously, a prophecy of his own untimely fate in
his poetic tragedy, "When the Dawn is Come"
(1908), and in a poem revealing his vision of the
poet leading Ireland on to victory in her fight for
national freedom. Like A. E. and Lionel Johnson, MacDonagh identified his vision of mystic
beauty with the Ireland of his dreams, expressing
in its finest essence the spirit of nationality that
is one of the fundamental ideals of the Celtic
Dawn.

Seumas MacManus, author of "Ballads of a
Country Boy" (1902), is better known as a re-
teller of old folk-tales. His "In Chimney Corners" (1899), "Through the Turf Smoke" (1899),
and "Donegal Fairy Stories" (1900), reveal a
spirit as racy of the soil and the life that he knows
and loves as that of any shanachie among the
cabins in the bleak northwest of Ireland. His
love of Ireland and his understanding of the Irish
mind, and the beautiful expression that he has
given to its dreams of the otherworld are reëchoed
in the work of another poet who, like MacManus,
has become a resident of the United States.
Norreys Jephson O'Connor has written in "Beside the Blackwater" (1914) of his love for the

grey mist-laden Irish landscape, and in his play,
"The Lennan Sidhe" (1916) of the faery life with
which that landscape is instinct.

The latest of the younger choir of Irish poets to
have achieved fame is Francis Ledwidge. His
brief biography contains all the essentials of
romance. Born in Slane, County Meath, he has
been a grocery clerk, a miner, a farmer, a dabbler
in hypnotism, and, at the present writing, is at
the front in the Balkans. Unlike Colum or
Stephens or MacGill, he has not chosen to express
anything of the life of the peasant. His verse,
"Songs of the Fields" (1916), is concerned only
with the celebration of beauty in nature. It is
neither symbolic, mystical, nor introspective; it
is joyous, exuberant, beautifully cadenced, and
betrays an intuitive feeling for the image-making
value of words. Poetic vision and an instinctive
inevitability of phrasing render it distinguished
above all recent Irish poetry. To many, especially in these days when poetry is being more
often wrought from the horror than from the
beauty of life, Ledwidge's verse will have the
haunting appeal of those who, like Theocritus,
sang of three perfect experiences that cannot be
banished from the world: youth, love and nature.

For he is preëminently the idyllic poet of our day, the singer of the open, wind-swept fields, the lover of nature in all the infinite variety of her beauty, in all her abundant store of color and music.

"I love the wet-lipped wind that stirs the hedge,
 And kisses the bent flowers that drooped for rain,
That stirs the poppy on the sun-burned ledge
 And like a swan dies singing without pain,
The golden bees go buzzing down to stain
 The lilies' frills, and the blue harebell rings,
And the sweet blackbird in the rainbow sings.

"Deep in the meadow I would sing a song,
 The shallow brook my tuning fork, the birds
My masters; and the boughs they hop along
 Shall mark my time: but there shall be no words
For lurking Echo's mock; an angel herds
 Words that I may not know, within, or you,
Words for the fabled meet, the good and true."

The poetry produced by the Celtic renascence has followed three tendencies. The movement influenced by Yeats seems, at this distance from its inception, a belated off-shoot of Preraphaelitism. Yeats himself has turned from poetry to the drama, has published a definitive edition of his works, and has produced little during the past few years. In his later work he has dwelled less often in the land of the imagination, and more frequently dealt with reality. The movement toward symbolism was standardized and bereft of its beauty, and has died away. A. E. has devoted his attention to social reform, and the agricultural movement has drawn him away from poetry. The revolt of the younger poets has been in the direction of realism on the one hand, and a concern with nature on the other. And, with the rise of a native drama, poetry has been relegated to a secondary place in the attention of Irish writers. Symbolism and mysticism, the exploration of legend, and the search for a refuge from the facts of life in art were the path of the elder generation. The new generation, as we shall see in the discussion of the drama and the novel, has turned the conditions and relations of every day life.

One theme, however, has been common to all the poets that we have discussed with the exception of William Sharp. All of them have been concerned with the awakening of a race-consciousness in Ireland, and all of them have expressed an abiding devotion to the aspiration of nationality and to the spiritual renascence whereby they have hoped to encompass it. This national ideal, fundamental in the thought that produced the renascencè itself, has received many interpretations and many varied expressions. With Yeats and A. E., with Lionel Johnson and Thomas Mac-Donagh, it has been identified with a vision of spiritual life and spiritual beauty, and it has taken the visible clothing of symbols drawn from the heroic legends of the past. In the work of those poets who have revolted from what they felt to be a tenuous ideal seeking refuge in the past, it has been productive of a criticism of modern Irish life. In the work of Synge and of Stephens this criticism has been emphasized by trenchant satire; in the work of Colum and Patrick MacGill it has been evidenced in a deep concern with the realities of existence. But the critical spirit of the new generation of Irish poets has been directed toward the awakening of a people to their ideals and to the destiny that is theirs if they will but labor at the reconstruction of their life. And it has been inspired by the one hope to which all the writers of the Celtic Dawn have given instinctive allegiance, the passionate hope of national independence.

CHAPTER IV

THE DRAMA

IT was during the late eighties and early nineties of the last century that a revival of interest in the arts of the theater began to evidence itself in England. Two of the contributing forces that operated in creating a more serious attitude toward the drama were the translations of the plays of Ibsen, and the foundation of the Independent Theater. The plays of Ibsen, and later those of other continental dramatists, set literary men to thinking of the drama as an essentially social force embodying a philosophic reaction to life in terms of social criticism, and as such an almost wholly new literary form in which to express themselves. They felt that the theater offered them a wider audience than they could ever hope to reach with the printed page, and therefore that the drama was the most democratic of the arts and the most direct in its appeal. They began to discuss the function of the theater, and to hope for a drama which, besides revealing a serious reading of life, would be graced, like that of Ibsen, by literary distinction. Their activities took tangible form in the foundation of the Independent Theater, an association formed with the purpose of producing plays that would not have obtained a hearing in the "commercial" theater. In their anxiety to approach life directly and reflect it accurately, the new playwrights wrote very realistic plays, making their appeal rather to the intellect than to the emotions of the audience. In the meanwhile the technique of production succumbed to a similar wave of realism; it was found consistent with the naturalism of the plays themselves to exactly reproduce the environment of life, and the minute and detailed naturalism of production against which there is so strong a revolt today was ubiquitous, both in the "commercial" and in the "intellectual" theater.

Naturalism in content and in production became the prevailing mode of the day in the theater, and almost immediately there came a reaction in the direction of symbolism, the best known exponent of which was Maurice Maeterlinck. Symbolism attached itself to the poetic drama, and the "modern movement" in the drama divided into two factions, one of which adhered to the tradition of naturalism and the play of intellect, inherited from Ibsen, and the other giving its allegiance to the poetic play. To this confusion as to the aims of the theater and the theory of the drama as an art, the Irish dramatic movement, as we shall presently see, owed its inception. First, however, it is necessary to briefly review a little of its early history.[1]

The primary impulse toward the establishment of a theater of art in Dublin came from William Butler Yeats. In 1885 he had composed "The Island of Statues," a pastoral dramatic poem, and in the following year "Mosada," a poetic tragedy of the Spanish Inquisition; both of which, although published in the earlier editions of his verse, have been rejected and do not appear in the "Collected Works" (1908). Between 1892 and 1899 he

[1] Two entertaining accounts are given in George Moore's "Ave," Heinemann, 1911, and Lady Gregory's "Our Irish Theatre," Putnam, 1913. See also W. B. Yeats, "The Irish Dramatic Movement," Vol. IV, Collected Works, "Ideas of Good and Evil," "The Work of the Abbey Theatre" in Plays, Macmillan. Weygandt's "Irish Plays and Playwrights," Houghton-Mifflin, is a survey of the Irish theater until 1913. See also "Samhain," and its predecessors "Beltaine" and "The Arrow," a yearly review published by The Abbey and edited by W. B. Yeats.

wrote "The Land of Heart's Desire," "The
Countess Cathleen," and a version of "The
Shadowy Waters," his favorite and most consid-
ered work, which was published in 1900. Only
"The Land of Heart's Desire" reached production, having been given at the Avenue Theater in
London in 1894. In 1899 Edward Martyn wrote
two plays, "The Heather Field" and "Maeve,"
which he found it impossible to have produced
in London, and which he thought of offering to
German managers for translation and production.
It was finally arranged, with the help of Lady
Gregory and of George Moore, to produce two
plays in Dublin. An English company was gathered and rehearsed in London, and on May 8th
and 9th, 1899, Yeats's "The Countess Cathleen"
and Martyn's "The Heather Field" were given
in the Antient Concert Rooms in Dublin. These
productions were made under the auspices of The
Irish Literary Theater, founded by Yeats, Martyn
and Lady Gregory with the hope of "building up
a Celtic and Irish school of dramatic literature."
The society planned for an experimental Spring
season in Dublin each year for three years. The
second season, at the Gaiety Theater, brought
forward Alice Milligan's "The Last Feast of the

Fianna," "The Bending of the Bough," which George Moore had adapted from Martyn's "The Tale of a Town," and Martyn's "Maeve." F. R. Benson assumed the burdens of the third series of productions, which consisted of "Diarmuid and Grania," an heroic play in prose by Yeats and Moore in collaboration, and "Casad-an-Sugan" (The Twisting of the Rope) a one act play in Gaelic by Dr. Douglas Hyde founded upon an episode in Yeats's "Stories of Red Hanrahan," the first play in Gaelic to be produced upon any stage. The three experimental years originally planned for having come to an end, William G. Fay and his brother, Frank J. Fay, associated themselves with Yeats and Lady Gregory and assumed the direction of a company of amateur actors who, as the Irish National Dramatic Company, gave performances in St. Teresa's Hall and in the Antient Concert Rooms during 1902. Their name was changed in the following year to The Irish National Theater Society which, in 1903 and 1904, gave performances in Molesworth Hall. In 1903 the company also gave two performances in London, which brought them to the attention of Miss A. E. F. Horniman, who purchased the Abbey Theater in Dublin, reconstructed it, and endowed the company for a period of six years. This service is but one of many benefactions that the modern English stage owes to Miss Horniman who, by her management of the Gaiety Theater in Manchester, has developed and encouraged all the arts of the theater in England. The Abbey Theater was opened on December 27th, 1904, with the first performance of Yeats's "On Baile's Strand." In 1905 the name of the company was changed to The National Theater Society, Ltd., which is the official title of the Abbey players.

The patent granted to the Abbey provides for the production of plays either written by Irishmen, or upon Irish subjects, or foreign masterpieces provided that they are not English. The restrictions thus set upon the company's activity have never interfered with the work of the Abbey, although the government has in several instances unsuccessfully threatened it, in an attempt to prevent the production of plays that were held to be morally or politically objectionable. The original group of players formed by the brothers Fay were recruited chiefly from the artisans of Dublin, and were unpaid, donating their services from a purely artistic motive. After the subsidy assured by Miss Horniman had been secured, pay-

ments were made to all members of the company,
in order that they might devote their entire time
to the work of the Abbey. Miss Horniman herself withdrew from the Abbey in 1910.

The Irish dramatic movement owed its inception, as we have said, to a reaction against the
naturalism of the commercial theater. Yeats
pointed out that in the modern play passion becomes sentimental, and that if the playwright
who deals with contemporary life is to be successful in the commercial theater he must deal only
with the surface of life. He saw that the French
playwrights had invented the play with a thesis
in order to project a serious criticism of life in the
drama, knowing that argument is almost the only
expression of passion in our daily life. He did
not believe, however, that art is concerned with
the expression of opinions that can be defended
by argument; what he desired was the upbuilding
of a school of Irish dramatists whose work would
contain either a vision or a criticism of life clothed
in beautiful language. He hoped that the race
consciousness of the Irish people would become
articulate in the work of a theater of art, and that
it would be the center of an intellectual and emotional tradition.

Since 1900, the date of publication of "The Shadowy Waters," the theater has occupied almost the entire time and attention of William Butler Yeats. His output of verse during the past sixteen years has been limited to two slim booklets, "In the Seven Woods" (1902), and the more recent "Responsibilities" (1915). In all he has written fifteen plays; the two of his youth have never been republished, and three others have been discarded. These are "Diarmuid and Grania," written in collaboration with George Moore, "The Pot of Broth," and "Where There Is Nothing." "The Hour Glass," a morality in prose first published in 1902, has been rewritten both as to text and idea and, although not included in the "Collected Works," has since been published in its amended version in "Responsibilities." His interest in the theater has also been productive of much critical writing, for the most part originally published in the occasional review issued by the Abbey of which he has been the editor, "Samhain" and its predecessors, "Beltaine" and "The Arrow." In the main, we are justified in saying that at the age of thirty-five William Butler Yeats closed his career as a lyric poet and turned his attention exclusively toward writing for the stage.

The qualities predominating in his lyric verse
are those most evident in the first three plays that
he wrote for the theater: "The Countess Cathleen" (1892–99), "The Land of Heart's Desire"
(1894), and "The Shadowy Waters" (1900).
Their beauty is that of atmosphere, of language,
of poetry symbolical of a spiritual life transcend-
ing the common actions of daily experience.   If
we remember that Yeats's object was to rid the
drama of what may be termed its theatricality,
to express in art the core and the spiritual essence
of life, the fact will serve to explain the apparent
absence of drama from the first versions of these
plays.   Like Maeterlinck, to whom in great part
he owes the development of his early dramatic
technique, Yeats oriented his material, stripped it
of all temporal allusion, and reduced it to the symbolical expression of the great aspirations and high
emotions that are constant in a life of changing
relations.

His dramatic method is founded upon certain
conceptions the most important of which are his
theories of comedy and tragedy, his theory of the
speaking of dramatic verse, and that of stage
decoration.   "Tragic art, passionate art," he has
written, "the drowner of dykes, the confounder

of understanding, moves us by setting us to rev-
erie, by alluring us almost to the intensity of
trance." The art of tragedy takes no account of
the individual distinction between man and man;
all that we mean by the term character is absent
from it, for its concern is with the universal and
the enduring in emotion, and it moves us by what
it brings us of our ideals, our visions and our
dreams. Comedy, on the other hand, has its
foundation in what Ben Jonson, and Congreve,
whom Yeats quotes, defined as humor; the predominating characteristic in the individual temperament by which its possessor is distinguished
from all other men. The tragedy and the drama
of poetry take us beyond ourselves and our daily
life, lifting us into an abstract world of ideal perfection, while our pleasure in comedy is dependent
upon a subtle discrimination in the values of our
daily life, the real world, finding its expression in
character.

This distinction between the mood of comedy
and that of tragedy in the play itself brought
Yeats to a realization of the necessity of its indication in the physical setting of the play. In
writing of the poetic play he has said: "If the real
world is not altogether rejected it is but touched

here and there, and into the places we have left
empty we summon rhythm, balance, pattern,
images that remind us of vast passions, the vague-
ness of past times, all the chimeras that haunt the
edge of trance." To create an atmosphere which
would convey the quality of this illusive mood by
employing the methods of decoration common to
the naturalistic drama was manifestly impossible.
He required a new art of decoration in which the
subtle play of light upon a conventionalized background should contribute atmosphere and emphasis to the mood of the spoken line through
allusion and suggestion rather than through a
photographically natural reproduction of concrete
reality. To secure this qualitative correspondence
between the dramatic poem and its physical background, Yeats summoned to his aid Gordon Craig,
with whom he had many ideas in common, and
who has since been recognized as the father of the
modern movement in scenic decoration. Together they developed a scheme in which the
decoration, although suggestive and evocative of
the mood of the drama, was completely subordinated to the action and the spoken line, functioning only as a background to them, and thus
never distracting the audience from concentra-

tion upon the play itself. A few of the designs
that Gordon Craig produced for the Abbey have
been published in the beautiful volume of "Plays
for an Irish Theater" issued by Mr. Bullen at the
Shakespeare Head Press at Stratford-upon-Avon
in 1911, and among them is the finely conceived
set employed in the production of "The Hour
Glass." The designs for the greater number of
Yeats's plays have, however, been the work of
Robert Gregory, Lady Gregory's son, a subscriber
to the theories of Yeats and Craig, and the composition of these sets has often been directly suggested by Yeats himself.

In establishing the hierarchy of the arts of the
theater for the Abbey, Yeats has placed the art
of the playwright preëminent, the art of the actor
second, and subordinate to both of these, the art
of the producer. Comment upon the acting of
the Abbey company is reserved for a later page,
but of one of the influences upon Yeats's dramatic
theory directly related to the art of acting some
account must be taken. On a previous page it
has been remarked that in 1902 Yeats resolved
to write all his long poems for the stage, and all
his short ones to be spoken to the psaltery. Just
how he came to this decision he has revealed in a

little essay upon "Speaking to the Psaltery" in "Ideas of Good and Evil." Both A. E. and Yeats had noticed that in composing their poems they had in mind certain definite notes which could be written down and played on the organ, as they discovered when they consulted Edward Martyn, or, in the case of Yeats's poems, "turned into something like a Gregorian hymn if one sang them in the ordinary way." Yeats then went to Arnold Dolmetsch, who made him an instrument akin to both the psaltery and the lyre, to the accompaniment of which Miss Florence Farr recited Yeats's verses, regulating her speech by the ordinary musical notation. This new method of elocution proved rich in rhythm and cadence, delicate in modulation and susceptible of an infinite nuance of expression. It was taught by Miss Farr to the Abbey company, and in accordance with it were recited all the songs and many of the lyric passages in Yeats's plays. In its effect it greatly resembles the beautiful art lately revealed to us in America by Madame Ratan Devi in her recitals of Hindu poetry. It has had a telling effect upon the diction of the Abbey players in their production of poetic drama; their speaking of verse is so fluent and liquid, so veri-

tably dramatic, that it makes much of the recitation of even great actors seem paltry and theatrical.

"The Countess Cathleen," "The Land of
Heart's Desire" and "The Shadowy Waters"
were followed by three plays in prose. "Diarmuid
and Grania" (1901) was written, as we said, in
collaboration with George Moore. It is probable
that the greater part of this play was the work of
Moore; the only part of it to reach publication is
a bit of the second act, written in French, and published in "Ave" (1911). The original plan by
which it was hoped to bring the play to maturity
has been amusingly described by Moore in "Ave."
He, it seems, was to write the play in French,
which was to be rendered into English by Lady
Gregory. Taidgh O'Donoghue was to translate
this version into Irish, which was to be retrans-
lated into English by Lady Gregory, and upon
this final version Yeats was to "put style." This
process, which Moore termed literary lunacy,
terminated in a failure. But it served to illustrate the function of the literary theater. The
heroic legend was conceived in terms of folk-
character, and the play itself was essentially a
literary play. Neither of the collaborators was

willing to give the play to the other for revision, and since George Moore's final desertion of the Irish movement, and the publication in 1912 of Lady Gregory's "Grania," it has seemed more than ever unlikely that the play will ever again reach the public.

"Cathleen ni Houlihan" (1902) is perhaps the best prose play that Yeats has written, and because of the patriotism of its allegory has proven the most popular of his works in Ireland. The legend of the fate-ridden old woman for whom men die and who, having lost her "four beautiful green fields," never despairs nor grows truly old, furnished him one of the most poetic themes in all the range of his work. There is to be found in this play a dialogue that is veritably dramatic; the greatest economy of means and of language has been sought for by the author, and the result is a finely wrought little masterpiece of drama. The character of Cathleen was probably suggested to Yeats by that of the old peasant woman, Peg Inerny, whose dual existence as a peasant by day and a queen of the Sidhe by night is chronicled in Edward Martyn's "Maeve." "The Pot of Broth" (1902), which followed "Cathleen," is a one act farce in the vein of Lady Gregory's writing, written in collaboration with Lady Gregory, and composed chiefly to demonstrate that Yeats's powers were not restricted to serious plays. It has been given with some success by W. G. Fay in the United Kingdom and in America.

"Where There Is Nothing" (1903) was probably influenced by Synge's "The Tinker's Wedding" which, although never produced by the Abbey company, had been written during the preceding year. Yeats's play deals with a gentleman and a scholar who joins a band of tinkers, revolting against what its author has called "the despotism of fact," and who dies an outcast from society in a vision of truth. As produced by the Stage Society in London in 1904 it scored no great success and failed to please Yeats, who relinquished the theme to Lady Gregory. She rewrote it as "The Unicorn from the Stars" in 1907, changing the character of the hero from an aristocrat to a coach-builder, and relieving the improbability of his death by also causing him to be an epileptic. In its original form the play comes very close to being autobiographical statement, and one can easily believe that the character of Paul Ruttledge figures forth one phase at least of Yeats's mind. In it one finds that revolt of the artist against a materialistic civilization, that firm belief in the truth of vision which is present in his early lyric verse, in "The Shadowy Waters," and, in a somewhat modified form, in "The King's Threshold." "The Hour Glass," a morality play of the same year, is concerned with a Wise Man who has destroyed Heaven and Purgatory with his knowledge, and with them the belief of the people in God. He is intimidated by an Angel and is taught belief by a Fool, who in so doing saves the Wise Man's soul. Recently, in "Responsibilities" (1915), the play has been rewritten, and the Wise Man is no longer taught truth by the Fool, but rather by the logic of circumstance. The influence to which the composition of "The Hour Glass" is usually attributed is "Everyman," which had been produced in London during the previous year. In theme it echoes the conflict between rationalism and intuition with which Yeats has been so greatly preoccupied. It illustrates the opposition of the world of experience which can be demonstrated by fact, and the world of belief that is revealed in vision; a polarity that is characteristic in one form or another of all of his writing.

The prose plays make evident, to a very large

degree, Yeats's acknowledged collaboration with
Lady Gregory, who, as he writes, taught him
"the true countenance of country life." The instinctive expression of himself, however, is in the
poetic tragedies. "On Baile's Strand" (1903),
is a beautiful setting of the tale, retold by Lady
Gregory in "Cuchulain of Muirthemne" (1902),
of the slaying by Cuchulain of the son of Aoife
whom he does not know to be his own. This
tragic legend, common to the folk-lore of all people, is set, in Yeats's version, in high relief against
the ironic characters of the Blind Man and the
Fool, who could, if they would, prevent the
tragedy, but do not, for the clash of arms gives
them the opportunity to rob the houses of the
people. The author himself has criticized this
play on the score of its complexity of plot; it was
to have been one of a cycle of plays devoted to
Cuchulain, but the others, with the exception of
"The Golden Helmet" (1910), have never been
written. It has true dramatic value, is ennobled
by distinguished, if not great, poetry, and the
manner of its setting forth is more direct and less
complex than that of the earlier poetic plays. It
was followed, in 1904, by "The King's Threshold,"
which many take, with "The Shadowy Waters,"

as containing both a purely personal expression
of Yeats's philosophy and his defence of his art.
The play deals with the old belief that a scorned
poet may defeat a king. Yeats chose for his plot
the middle Irish legend of the poet, Seanchan,
who, having been deprived of his seat at the king's
high table, stands at the king's threshold to starve
to death. For there was a belief that a dishonored
poet, should he starve on the threshold of those
who have insulted him, even though it be a king,
would bring a curse on the house. Finally
Seanchan triumphs, and the king offers him the
crown:

> "Kneel down, kneel down; he has the greater power.
> There is no power but has its roots in his—
> I understand it now. There is no power
> But his that can withhold the crown or give it,
> Or make it reverent in the eyes of men,
> And therefore I have laid it in his hands,
> And I will do his will."

To which Seanchan replies:—

> "O crown! O crown!
> It is but right the hands that made the crown
> In the old time should give it where they please.
> O silver trumpets! Be you lifted up,

And cry to the great race that is to come.
Long-throated swans, amid the waves of Time,
Sing loudly, for beyond the wall of the world
It waits, and it may hear and come to us!"

The final speech of Seanchan, it is interesting to note, is the first indication in Yeats's published work that a change has come over his art and that it no longer seeks refuge in dreaming over the past, but confidently looks "to the great race that is to come." The play is written out of as definite an experience as is any of Yeats's published work. At the time of its composition the newspapers had called into question the honesty of his motives in producing Synge's "In the Shadow of the Glen" at the Abbey, and his fellow Nationalists were asserting that Yeats cared more for his art than he did for the Irish people. Criticism and obloquy poured in on him from a public exercised by journalistic agitation against Synge and the Abbey, and from politicians and students who resented his growing concern with art. His answer to the critics of both quarters is contained in "The King's Threshold." Conceived less truly in terms of drama than "On Baile's Strand," it is perhaps the most eloquently beautiful statement of the power of poetry and the value to society of the poet that has been made in our day.

Yeats's chief contribution to the modern poetic drama is "Deirdre" (1906), a play of haunting loveliness and of truly great poetry. This most poignant of the "Three Sorrows of Story Telling" is also the most famous and the most beautiful of Celtic folk-tales, and few Irish writers from Sir Samuel Ferguson on have not made it the subject of either poem or play. In our own day plays about Deirdre, whose legend is only less known than that of Iseult, have been written by A. E., Synge, Eva Gore-Booth, and Father Thomas O'Kelly. Yeats has adapted the legend to his own purposes, and concentrated as a focal point upon the meeting of Conchubar, Naisi and Deirdre in the guest house on the return of the lovers to Ireland. In thus compressing the tragedy within the limits of a single episode, he has immeasurably increased the dramatic power of the legend. A bold and effective stroke of dramatic technique is the psychological parallelism with which Yeats has invested his play. The action takes place in an old guest house in a wood, the very house in which Lughaidh Redstripe and his wife, who during half of the year had the body of a seamew, played at chess while they awaited death. Their story, like that of Deirdre and Naisi, is one of "treachery, a broken promise and a journey's end," the chess-board upon which they played is still in the house, and this lends to the actions of Deirdre, who suspects treachery on the part of Conchubar, an austere terror. The parallelism is both internal and external; it has a deliberate effect upon Deirdre, Naisi and Fergus, and it affords the audience both an ironic foreboding of the final tragedy and a sharp contrast between the cold woman of the sea, and the passionate, sensuous and untamed Deirdre. With the introduction of the chorus, approximated in the characters of the Fool and the Blind Man in "On Baile's Strand," but consummated in "Deirdre" by the three women musicians, the poet achieved the difficult task of writing a tragedy in which the Greek and the modern spirit have been successfully blended. It is the only play by Yeats that has had conspicuous success in any theater other than the Abbey when not given by the Abbey players; the part was rewritten for Mrs. Patrick Campbell, who added it to her repertoire and played it in London and Dublin with the Abbey company in 1907-8, and also with a company of her own. "Deirdre" is the most effective of his plays in the theater because, of all his plays, it is written with the surest eye to conventional dramatic construction and to the resources of the theater itself; its dramatic appeal is, however, as greatly due to the beautiful content of the story as to excellences of construction and craftsmanship. And in clothing the content of his play with a potent and wistfully beautiful lyricism, Yeats has justified his theory of the theater.

The note of "Deirdre" is that of two earlier plays, "The Land of Heart's Desire" and "The Shadowy Waters." It embodies Yeats's most characteristic theme as a poet-dramatist; that of the right of men and women to life. In the earlier plays the life sought is one of the spirit, a refuge in dream from the daily round of existence. In "Deirdre," however, it is actual experience as we know it, that is desired; although the terms in which it is set transcend the common life, they are but its quintessence. The two plays that he has written since "Deirdre" have contributed nothing to his art; "The Golden Helmet" (1910), a legendary farce written in heroic couplets, is but a reworking of "The Green Helmet" (1908),

and neither of them marks an advance over his
previous writing, nor has either achieved any
success.

The chief characteristic of the folk-lore of primitive peoples is its indwelling love of magic, and to
this Celtic legend is no exception. We have seen
how Yeats's belief in magic and his theories of the
occult affected his lyric verse; it is more difficult,
perhaps, to understand how he has reconciled
with the modern mind this love of magic, either
as an interpretation or a symbolism of experience,
in the drama, which is necessarily more explicit
than the lyric.   In all of his plays, however, even
those which are not directly founded upon folk-
tales, there is no experience which cannot be interpreted as having occurred through the agency
of magic, and in this Yeats evidences his fidelity
to the psychology of legend. We have, in "The
Shadowy Waters," Forgael winning the love of
Dectora by a magic spell; in "Deirdre," Deirdre
herself compels the love of men and sets Ireland
at war through her magical beauty, and Conchubar plans to win her by magic; in "The Land of
Heart's Desire" it is the magic of vision that lures
Mary Bruin to her death, while in "The Countess
Cathleen" the magic of evil is overcome by an

equally potent spell, the magic of perfect faith. If, as we like to believe, the modern mind has accepted science as an interpretation of experience, how is it that these fables contain the quality of inevitability? Perhaps it is because the plays take us to a world out of time and out of space in which all things are possible; perhaps it is because the imagination even of the modern mind finds in magic a symbolic interpretation of spiritual forces whose potency has found no other explanation; perhaps we, like the musicians in "Deirdre," and like Yeats himself have

" . . . wild thought
Fed on extravagant poetry and lit
By such a dazzle of old fabulous tales
That common things are lost, and all that's strange
Is true because 'twere pity if it were not."

or perhaps it is because, with Plato, we believe that there resides in surpassing beauty a compelling spiritual power.

The work of the other founders of the Irish dramatic movement is overshadowed by that of Yeats. George Moore began his career as a playwright with "The Strike at Arlingford" (1893) and his incursion into the dramatic field was attended by a curious circumstance. In "Im-

·pressions and Opinions" (1891) Moore had se-
verely criticized all the contemporary English
playwrights, and so offended one of them, G. R.
Sims, a writer of melodrama, that Sims offered
to pay a hundred pounds for a stall to witness an
unconventional play by George Moore. Moore
accepted the challenge, after insisting upon the
withdrawal of the word "unconventional" since,
were the word retained, he would have to abide
by Sims's definition of unconventionality in dramatic art. "The Strike at Arlingford" was the
result of the challenge, and its production by the
Independent Theater, besides being an event of
some journalistic importance, brought Moore a
cheque of a hundred pounds from Sims. The play
itself does not seem, in the perspective of twenty-
three years, either unconventional or essentially
novel in theme or treatment. It was obviously
written under the influence of Ibsen, and unlike
the plays of Ibsen, its characters do not seem pro-
jected into life, but arbitrarily constructed. In
the following year Moore collaborated with Mrs.
Craigie ("John Oliver Hobbes") upon "Journeys
End in Lovers' Meetings," and five years later
was prevailed upon by his cousin, Edward Martyn,
to assist in the production of Martyn's "The

Heather Field." In 1899 Moore had already achieved a notable reputation as a novelist and critic, while his quarrel with Sims and his connection with the Independent Theater made him considered something of an authority upon the drama. It is therefore obvious that Yeats and Martyn, planning the future of an Irish literary theater, and practically inexperienced in the drama, should have had recourse to a well-known writer whose intellectual curiosity would tempt him to subscribe to their theories, and who happened also to be a prominent member of the Irish aristocracy.

During 1900, Martyn's "The Tale of a Town," written for the Irish Literary Theater, was rejected by Moore and Yeats, and Martyn, with rare unselfishness, gave it to Moore for revision. Moore rewrote it as "The Bending of the Bough" (1900) and under this title it was successfully given during the company's second season. As Moore wrote it, the play turned out to be a satire upon Irish political life that, as Lady Gregory has written, "hits impartially all round." It was the first play dealing with a vital question in modern Irish life to be produced by what later came to be the Abbey company, and for that reason, as the

pioneer of the realistic school in Ireland, it is of
historic importance. The play is concerned with a
politician, Jasper Dean, who betrays the interests
of his constituents in order to please his fiancée.
Martyn had laid his scene in Ireland, but Moore,
in order, perhaps, to avoid charges of libel, trans-
ferred it to Scotland, making the allegory sufficiently thin to enable the point to penetrate even
the most thick-skinned Irish partisan. It is effective as satire, although hardly, apart from its
incisiveness as a study of Irish affairs, of any
especial significance as a contribution to the contemporary drama. Of "Diarmuid and Grania"
sufficient has already been said. Moore broke
with the dramatic movement following its production, and contented himself with pamphleteering
in favor of the Abbey. "The Apostle,"[1] published in 1911, is a scenario for a play on the life of
Christ preceded by a "letter upon reading the
Bible for the first time." In this study, Moore has
represented the meeting of Jesus and of Paul in an
Essene monastery some years after the Crucifixion;
Jesus disapproves of the legend that has grown up
around his name, he is the simple carrier of water

---

[1] It is reported that "The Apostle" has served as a basis
for Moore's forthcoming novel, "The Brook Kerith."

and hewer of logs, the shepherd, in a community in whose scholastic disputations he takes no part. When Paul, the mystic, the prophet, the demagogue comes into the community, and tells the Essenes of the gospel of Christianity, Jesus is shocked to find that his vision has become a cult held by people who have missed its profoundest meaning. When the identity of Jesus is disclosed to Paul, Paul believes himself the victim of an hallucination of the Devil, and when Jesus is recognized by Mary Magdalene, now an old woman, Paul strikes him down, believing him an impostor, and goes forth on his way to Rome. The play, should it ever come to be written, will, if one may judge its probable qualities by those of the scenario, possess a high degree of dramatic interest, and will differ from the many modern plays in which Christ figures, in that it presents Christ as essentially human; a visionary, a poet, and the prophet of a spiritual democracy.

"Elizabeth Cooper" (1913), founded upon an amorous missive received by Moore, which suggested the possibility of an adventure that the author assures us remained unrealized, is a little comedy of love and mistaken identity. It was produced by the Incorporated Stage Society in

London in 1913. A dramatization of "Esther Waters" produced by the Stage Society in the previous year earned little praise from either critics or audience. Moore has not become an outstanding figure in the contemporary drama chiefly because it is an art which he has not studied as carefully nor evolved as thoroughly as that of the novel; dramatic expression seems to have been merely an incidental by-product of his long experience as a writer, and it is probable that he has not taken it very seriously.

Edward Martyn has, however, been conscientious and serious in all his efforts as a playwright. His earliest essay in that form, "Morgante the Leper," a "satiric romance," was published anonymously in 1890. He was known in Ireland as a wealthy landlord, an amateur in music, a deeply religious supporter of the Catholic Church, and a Nationalist in so far as he had any political convictions. In all he has written six plays: "Maeve" and "The Heather Field" in 1899, "The Tale of a Town" in 1900, "The Enchanted Sea" in 1902, "The Place Hunters" in 1905, and "Grangecolman" in 1912. Occasionally, though very infrequently, he has written brief articles in "Samhain" in explanation of his ideas of the theater, none of which are as revealing as the plays themselves. Just after the refusal of the three other directors to produce his "The Tale of a Town," he severed his connection with the theater. Soon afterward, when the policy of the movement had crystallized, and the company was committed to the production of folk-plays and plays dealing with contemporary Irish peasant life, Martyn gave ten thousand pounds to the Catholic Pro-Cathedral of Dublin wherewith to establish a Palestrina choir, thus putting a definite end to the hope that he would endow a theater of art.

In so far as his work is founded upon a tradition, Edward Martyn is a follower of Ibsen, and the dependence of his work upon that of the Norwegian playwright is singularly close, both in the realm of ideas and in the technique of their expression. He stands in opposition to the theory of the peasant drama and to the use of the peasant dialect as a medium of artistic expression. His plays are chiefly drawn from the life of the middle and upper classes; only one character in all his plays, that of Peg Inerny in "Maeve," belongs to the peasantry, and she is rather a symbol of Ireland than an individualized type. It can be readily understood from what has been said, at the opening of this chapter, of the differences existing between the ideas of the Abbey group and the prevailing theory of the drama in the late nineties, that Martyn's theories were out of harmony with those of the other directors.

The obviously fine quality of his two best plays, "Maeve" and "The Heather Field" is the beauty of idea. The first of these is dramatically conceived, and in its high moments instinct with passionate emotional expression. "Maeve," also, is replete with unrealized poetry. Both plays are studies in the contrast between spiritual and actual life, in which the splendor of dream and of vision, irreconcilable with the petty miseries of reality, are the lure to final destruction. Both plays evidence a telling symbolism; Carden Tyrell, who goes mad when his little son brings him a sprig of heather from the mountain which he has set his heart upon reclaiming, and Peg Inerny, the peasant woman who is a servitor by day, and a queen of the Sidhe by night, are equally figuring forth that contest between vision and reality which plays so great a part in the Irish mind and in the work of the modern Irish writers.

The plays that follow these are relatively unimportant; "The Tale of a Town" is a failure

from the point of view of the theater, "The Place
Hunters" crude farce, "The Enchanted Sea" an
Ibsenesque melodrama, and "Grangecolman"
social criticism of no very great illumination or
insight. One great defect in Martyn's art is his
inability to realize feminine character. His dialogue, too, is, except in rare instances of lyric
enthusiasm, labored and stiff, and conveys no
illusion of actual conversation. For this reason
his characters, although the underlying conception is always very powerful, are deficient in veri-
similitude. He conceives character in terms of
ideas rather than in terms of emotion, and where
emotion is present in his plays, it is quite likely
to be cold and hard. Had he been willing, like
Yeats, to study the dramatic technique of other
writers, he would have probably been the accepted
chronicler of one phase of Irish life, that of the
decaying gentry, the politicians and the priests.
As it stands, he is a failure as a dramatist, but a
failure who has enriched literature with one beautiful play, "The Heather Field," and an only less
perfect play, "Maeve," an exquisite fancy to
which Yeats owes the inspiration of "The Countess
Cathleen."

Lady Gregory has been the most prolific writer

of those who founded the Abbey movement. She
has written twenty-one plays, five volumes of
prose, and seven translations from the dramatic
literatures of other nations. She has been assid-
uous in the collection of dialect in the village of
Kiltartan in Galway, and it is in this idiom that
she has written her plays, translations, and "Cuchulain of Muirthemne" (1902). In addition to
this, she has lectured on Irish literary ideals and
on the work of the Abbey before many audiences,
has written controversial articles, and acted in a
managerial capacity both in Dublin and on the
frequent tours made by the company. Many of
her plays were written during a transient period of
decline in the production of dramatic material, in
order that the activity of the company might
continue without interruption. She began as a
writer of comedy, of plays, which, as she writes,
"Lady Gregory calls comedy, and everyone else,
farce," because a contrast to the poetic tragedies
of Yeats was the material most urgently required
during the early years of the theater. Her reputation as a playwright very largely depends upon
these comedies, and it is the genre with which her
name has chiefly been associated. Her plays
are built upon a slender thread of material, in-

sufficient for the creation of a truly enduring drama, they illustrate no conflict of will, purpose, or passion; they lack the subtle discrimination and the fine selective sense of the thoroughly trained dramatist. They are, however, facile, often witty, the record of a gossipy mind conscious of its intellectual superiority to the picturesque incongruities of the life that it has accurately observed. Her best work has been done in comedy because her talent is for externalized situation, but drama, with Lady Gregory, is almost invariably subordinated to the interest in idiom and folk-legend. With the advent of Synge, Lady Gregory began to write plays of a more serious nature, and the fruit of this labor has been her two volumes of "Irish Folk-History Plays" (1912) and "The Goal Gate," (1906), "The Rising of the Moon" (1907), a little morality play, "The Travelling Man" (1910), and "MacDarragh's Wife" (1912). Her finest achievements in the three veins in which she has written have been "The Canavans" (1906), a comedy of folk-history written out of her knowledge of the peasantry; "The Image" (1909), another play of peasant life, which, under the guise of comedy, is a serious indictment of the disposition to accept as a certainty the remote possibility of an event that may never be realized; and "The Goal Gate," a powerful and beautiful little tragedy in the lives of two peasant women. With a knowledge of these plays it becomes increasingly difficult to give any serious attention to the earlier farces as representing an important contribution to the dramatic writing of our time. They were written to order, possess a certain effectiveness when staged and interpreted by the Abbey Company, and are sufficiently obvious in their presentation of life to demand little or no reflective consideration of their philosophic content.

Both the other founders of the Irish literary revival have given some attention to the drama. Dr. Hyde's work has, for the most part, been done in Gaelic: "The Twisting of the Rope" (1901), "Nativity Play" (1911) and "The Tinker and the Fairy" have delighted many audiences with their beauty. "The Lost Saint" (1912), "The Bursting of the Bubble" (1903), "The Marriage" (1911) and "The Poorhouse" (1903), written in collaboration with Lady Gregory, have all scored some success. "The Poorhouse" has since its production been discarded by Dr. Hyde, and rewritten by Lady Gregory as "The Work-

house Ward" (1908). The sole contribution to
the drama made by A. E. has been "Deirdre," a
three act play in prose, written at the request of
the Fays and produced with Yeats's "Cathleen
ni Houlihan" in 1902. The play is poetic in its
conception, written in an almost chiselled prose,
but it fails as vital drama, although the qualities
of its beauty are abundant. Neither A. E. nor
Dr. Hyde can be considered essentially dramatic
writers, although the influence of the one led
directly to the "Deirdre of the Sorrows" of
Synge; and that of the other has been felt in every
folk-play that has been written in Ireland since
the late nineties.

With the production, on October 8th, 1903, of
"In the Shadow of the Glen," a new name, destined to become the most widely known of those
connected with the literature of modern Ireland,
appeared on the playbills of the Irish National
Theatre Society. John Millington Synge [1] was
born in 1871, at Rathfarnham, near Dublin. As

[1] The standard authority on Synge is Maurice Bourgeois,
"John M. Synge and the Irish Theatre," Constable and Co.,
Ltd., London, 1913. See also W. B. Yeats, "Synge and the
Ireland of His Time," Cuala Press, 1911; Masefield, "Dic-
tionary of National Biography," 2d Supp., Vol. III. "Con-
temporary Review," April, 1911; "John M. Synge," by John

a child he lived much in County Wicklow, learned
to speak Irish, was a student of music, and spent
most of his time tramping the Wicklow mountains,
learning about birds and trees. He graduated
from Trinity College, Dublin, and went to Germany with some idea of becoming a professional
musician. His aims seem to have been somewhat chaotic; he was at this time well versed in
both Irish and Hebrew, in which languages he had
taken prizes at Trinity, and he studied the theory
as well as the practice of music. From Germany
he went to Paris, and, during the next few years,
travelled, notably in Italy. He gave up the idea
of being anything more than an amateur of music,
and devoted himself to the study of French, doing
desultory literary criticism and some journalism.
He studied ancient Irish at the College de France,
joined a Young Ireland Society in Paris, and, in
1898, met William Butler Yeats. To Yeats must
be given the credit of having discovered the most
discussed of Irish playwrights. He had just
spent a day on the Aran Islands, whither he per-

Masefield; Lady Gregory, "Our Irish Theatre," Maunsel,
Dublin, 1913. This list is confined to extended treatment
by those who knew Synge. Mr. Bourgeois' volume has the
advantage of having been officially approved by the Synge
family.

suaded Synge to go, telling him of the primitive
life there, and encouraging him to seek a literary
reputation in Ireland by forewarning him of his
failure to attain success as a critic of French
literature.   Synge went to Aran later in the year,
and subsequently made two other visits.   He
also travelled through Wicklow and Kerry, and
through the congested districts of Connemara,
at a later date, and wrote his impressions of them.
He became one of the little group that was trying
to foster the development of a national drama,
and was actively associated in the management
of the Abbey from its opening, in 1904.   By this
time two plays of his had already been produced: "In the Shadow of the Glen" in 1903, and
"Riders to the Sea" in 1904.   Both had been
written in 1902, as had also "The Tinker's Wedding," which has not yet been produced in Ireland.   "The Well of the Saints," written in 1904,
was produced in 1905; "The Playboy of the Western World," written in 1906, was produced in 1907.
"Deirdre of the Sorrows" upon which he was at
work until the day of his death, March 24th, 1909,
was produced as he had left it, in 1910.   The
first two plays are in one act, the third in two acts,
and the following three all in three acts.

There exists in the work of Synge the not unusual correspondence between a delicate physical organization and a taste for the heightened emotional activity of contest with the rough and turbulent elementary forces from which it is precluded. In all of Synge's plays there is emphasized this aspiration to a wider personal experience of the passionate moments of life; it is the motivating force of all choice and activity; it is forced into relief with tragic intensity by the irony of circumstance that alone obstructs its progress. This theme of eagerness for a more impassioned life is largely the reflection of the man's personality; but he was fortunate enough to be able to choose his dramatic material from among a people in whom it is a predominating characteristic. He loved chiefly what was wild and primitive in Irish life; for the modern age of industrialism he had little sympathy, for he felt that it was robbing life of the quality of its zestful moments, and his dramatic instinct led him to value only the climaxes of high passion and bitter contest in an otherwise drab existence. Life transfigured by the imagination of a poet is the substance of his drama; he offers no solution, spiritual or moral, content merely with its faithful report.   His sole personal

comment lies in the ruthless irony which impreg-
nates, with the exception of "Riders to the Sea"
and "Deirdre," the whole of his art.   And in his
feeling that only in the quest of a wider experience
of life, intellectual, physical, and spiritual, can the
spirit of man attain emotional satisfaction, lies
whatever constructive philosophy is offered by his
art.   Synge, although he was the first dramatist
to construct a powerful play in the dialect of the
west, was not the first to employ that dialect.   It
had an earlier literary usage in the "Cuchulain of
Muirthemne" of Lady Gregory, and in Doctor
Hyde's translations, but Synge, writing of a life
that, in its external relations, is limited to a little
known locality in a language equally limited, was
the first to rise above the essential narrowness implicit in these limitations and construct a drama
of universal interest.   He labored incessantly
with the vehicle of his expression, adding, as he
learned, to its exuberance, to its fantasy, to its
poetry, and finally he attained that perfect harmony of form and content that is the index of
true art.

His theories of the art of the playwright are
stated in the prefaces to "The Tinker's Wedding,"
"The Playboy," and "Poems and Translations."

Primarily he reacted against the influence of
Yeats and the theories for which that poet stood.
Mysticism and an over accentuated spirituality
seemed to him to have little in common with the
life of the Irish peasant; the poetry of legend,
seeking a refuge from the experience of the common life, proved too remote from reality for one
to whom the standards of an art out of relation
with life were repellent. "On the stage," he wrote,
"one must have reality, and one must have joy;
and that is why the intellectual modern drama
has failed and people have grown sick of the false
joy of the musical comedy, that has been given
them in place of the rich joy found only in what is
superb and wild in reality." He rebelled also
against the didactic drama, the play of intellectual
problems, and an art concerned with propaganda.
"The drama, like the symphony, does not teach
or prove anything." His whole theory seems to
rest upon the assumption that the drama, if it is
to attain true poetic exaltation, must have its
roots firmly fixed in homely reality. And, finally,
the "drama is made serious not by the degree
with which it is taken up with problems that are
serious in themselves, but by the degree in which
it gives the nourishment, not very easy to define,

on which our imaginations live"; and chief among
the qualities which furnished this nourishment of
the imagination, Synge ranked humor.

In a little essay on "The Vagrants of Wicklow"
Synge has given a most complete account of his
conception of character, and the paragraph serves
so well as an explanation of his choice of subject-
matter that it may be quoted in full. "In all the
circumstances of this tramp life there is a certain
wildness that gives it romance and a peculiar
value for those who look at life in Ireland with an
eye that is aware of the arts also. In all the
healthy movements of art, variations from the
ordinary types of manhood are made interesting
for the ordinary man, and in this way only, the
higher arts are universal. Beside this art, however, founded upon the variations which are a
condition and effect of all vigorous life, there is
another art—sometimes confounded with it—
founded on the freak of nature, in itself a mere
sign of atavism or disease. This latter art, which
is occupied with the antics of the freak, is of interest only to the variation from ordinary minds and
for this reason is never universal. To be quite
plain, the tramp in real life, Hamlet and Faust in
the arts, are variations; but the maniac in real

life, and Des Esseintes and all his ugly crew in the
arts, are freaks only."

His art, indeed, is just as surely the art of the
variation as was that of Shakespeare or Goethe.
It would be difficult for a critic with a love for
classification to fit the spirit of Synge's plays into
any of the customary literary pigeon-holes. A
realist he undoubtedly was in that he founded his
art entirely upon reality of experience as he had
observed it.   On the other hand, his very cult of
the variation made him seek the unusual, and the
romantic episodes that are sharply delineated
from the common tenor of life prove him to a certain extent a romanticist.   It is difficult, also,
to reconcile to that profound irony of his art, the
intense joy in life that is one of its most prominent
characteristics.   Delight in nature, in the physical beauty of women, in the wild life of the roads
is joined with the consciousness of a very immi-
nent death.   But although Synge's view of life
was preëminently tragic, his only play in which
tragedy is the unrelieved and dominating mood,
"Riders to the Sea," is the least characteristic of
his writings.   Synge was a theorist neither about
art nor about morals, and in none of his plays is
there to be found any expression of the views of

their author. For these views the reader must
go to his two volumes of travel sketches, "The
Aran Islands" and "In Wicklow and West Kerry,"
and to his poems. These latter reveal him most
completely; in them there is the mordant irony,
the love of the grotesque, the sense of the brevity
and the incompleteness of life, the reaction against
the etiolated spiritual beauty cultivated by A. E.
and by Yeats, and the abiding love of nature and
of life that illuminate his plays. The travel note-
books contain the earliest indications of the back-
grounds of his plays. In their recreation of the
daily life of the peasantry, in their clear cut description, and even in the conversation recorded,
they illustrate the power of reproducing concrete
impressions that is one of the most important elements of Synge's dramatic instinct.

The question of Synge's fidelity to Irish life has
been debated more often with less profit than any
other purely literary question that has arisen out
of the work of the Abbey playwrights. One has
but to remember the tempestuous scenes that
greeted the first production of "The Playboy" in
Dublin in 1907 and in the United States in 1911
to appreciate the animosity aroused by his work
among certain groups of Irishmen. The decision

of the directors to retain the play despite all opposition was the turning point in the fortunes of the
theater. Had the directors succumbed to public
feeling, Synge would have remained an unknown
writer. The primary truth of his plays to Irish
life lies in their delineation of the conflict between
reality and the ideal which is characteristic of the
Celtic consciousness. Synge was neither the
first nor the only playwright of the Abbey group
to employ this theme; it is implicit in the work of
Yeats, and there it assumes an autobiographic
aspect; it has been satirized by Lady Gregory, and
conceived in a purely dramatic vein by many of
the younger writers. The chief infidelity of his
work to Irish life is, as M. Bourgeois has pointed
out, his total disregard of the religious life of the
people in a country where that phase of experience
plays almost the greatest individual role in the
daily life of the community.

Synge's plays have two analogues in literary
manner. On the one hand they resemble the
medieval French farces, and to a certain degree
the pungent raciness of Rabelais. On the other,
they partake of the nature and sophisticated
cynicism and irony of the novels of Anatole France.
We know that Synge was familiar with this ma-

terial, and it may be counted, just as the work of
Pierre Loti has been counted, an influence upon
his art.   But in the final analysis Synge is a clearly
original, and not a derivative writer.

His employment of the peasant idiom marks
the highest achievement in its use as a medium
of literary expression.   He amplified and enriched
the vocabulary that he had learned from his life
in Aran, and that which he had gleaned during
his life as a child among the Gaelic speaking
peasantry of Wicklow, making it ever more
poetic, more musical and more rhythmic.   It is
this last quality of rhythm that distinguishes his
work from all other contemporary prose, and
in which consists his innovation as a literary
artist.

The literary biography of Padraic Colum is
brief.   Two early plays concerned with folk-lore
and with medieval history failed to be either produced or published.   By 1902 he had written
and published four plays, one of which, "The
Saxon Shillin'", achieved success because of its
propagandist material.   All four plays, the other
three were entitled "The Kingdom of the Young,"
"The Foleys" and "Eoghan's Wife," dealt with
peasant life in the Irish midlands, of which he has

since become the chief chronicler. The following year marked his entrance and that of Synge
into the company of playwrights whose work has
been produced at the Abbey. His play was
"Broken Soil." It was his ambition at that time,
as he confesses in the preface to "Thomas Muskerry," to write in dramatic form a *comédie hu-
maine* of Irish life, and in a measure his subsequent work has been a partial fulfillment of that
desire. The production of "Broken Soil" convinced its author that revision of the text was de-
sirable, and the play was withdrawn, rewritten,
and produced four years later as "The Fiddler's
House." During the interval he wrote two other
plays, both of which were successfully produced,
"The Miracle of the Corn" in 1904, and "The
Land" in 1905. In 1907 he wrote "The Desert"
upon a theme later developed by Edward Knob-
lauch in "Kismet;" it would probably not have
been published had not "Kismet" scored a success during its Dublin production. In the same
year he published the two little stories which, with
a reprint of "The Miracle of the Corn," make up
the little booklet called "Studies." In 1909 appeared his volume of lyric verse, "Wild Earth,"
and in the following year he produced his two

most recent plays, "Thomas Muskerry" and "The Destruction of the Hostel."

With Padraic Colum the emphasis is placed upon situation rather than upon character or atmosphere, for, as he writes in the preface to "Thomas Muskerry": "The dramatist is concerned not primarily with the creation of character, but with the creation of situation. For character conceived as a psychological synthesis he has only a secondary concern. His main effort is always towards the creation of situations that will produce a powerful impression on an audience, for it is situation that makes the strongest appeal to our sympathies." He too, like Synge, and like many other dramatists of the modern school, is a regional playwright, but whereas Synge succeeded in compelling the interest of his audience in spite of an unfamiliar locale, Colum's locale does not create the play itself nor set the terms of its problem.

In the three plays of contemporary Irish life which he has written, the fundamental problem in each case arises from the life of the family, into which each member, actuated by self interest, has put his spiritual and physical energies, and in the effort to regain an independent existence, is confronted by another with a conflicting purpose. In "Thomas Muskerry" it is the grandfather who is sacrificed to the younger generation; in "The Land" it is the strong and the educated who desert the hardly won farm for the lure of America, leaving the soil to the witless and weak; in "The Fiddler's House" it is the father who, possessed with the soul of an artist, and imbued with the wanderlust, destroys both the home and the happiness of his elder daughter. The life of the family, although productive of dramatic situation, is not the sole generating cause of action in his plays. Love of land, of the road, the revolt of youth from tradition, and its decision to live its own life are the determining factors in the motivation of his plays.

In "The Land," which he characterizes as an "agrarian comedy," the action takes place during the operation of the Wyndham Act of 1903, which provided for the purchase by the peasantry of the land upon which they had been settled, but of which their tenure had previously existed only at the pleasure of the landlord. Martin Douras is a peasant with an education and a tendency of mind that unfit him for the agricultural life. In the gratification of his desire for intellectual calm, he has allowed his farm to be ruined by his windy and vacillating son, Cornelius, while his daughter, Ellen, who has received a convent education, has been influenced by the profitless life of her home to a disgust both with life on a farm, and with the life of a country schoolteacher for which she has been trained.   In love with her is Matt Cosgar, the son of Murtagh Cosgar, a well to do farmer, who at the opening of the play, has just completed the purchase of his farm.   Full of ambition for the future of his family, he quarrels with his son because of the love affair with Ellen, and forbids their marriage.   His disregard for the wishes of his children has already caused all but Matt and his witless sister Sally to emigrate to America.   Matt, having quarrelled with his father, finds his love for Ellen in conflict with the love that he has for the land, which is to be his if he will give up Ellen; finally, however, Ellen decides that, rather than be the wife of a farmer, she will emigrate to America, where there are crowds, where there is progress, where life has the quality of contest, and Matt, bidding defiance to his father, goes with her, sacrifices the life that he cares for at the moment when its opportunity is greatest, and allows the farm to pass to Sally and the incapable Cornelius. The tragedy lies with father and son, both having the same object at heart, equally implacable of purpose, both defeated.

"The Fiddler's House" is the tale of Conn Hourican, old in years and young in heart, who in former time had been a fiddler of renown, and a man of the roads, and who finds it difficult to settle down on the bit of a farm that his elder daughter, Maire, has inherited from her grandmother. The younger daughter, Anne, is domestic in her taste, loving quiet and peace, and the simple life of the farm, in contrast with which the dimly remembered life of the road seems a thing of horror. She is betrothed to James Moynihan, a youngster of poetic nature, whose father refuses to allow his marriage to a dowerless girl. Maire, however, is the child of her father, restive, excitable, but of firmer purpose; she has fallen in love with a tempestuous farmer named Brian MacConnel, and it is this love of which she is afraid. Finally, when her father has announced his intention of again taking to the road, she deeds the farm to her sister, who can then marry the man of her choice, and fearful lest her own love for Brian be too consuming, she leaves him, and goes off on the roads with her father.

"Thomas Muskerry" is the most powerful play of the three, for it deals with the dull monotony of existence in a small Irish town. Thomas Muskerry himself has for thirty years been master of the workhouse at Garrisowen, and intends to retire on his pension, purchase a small cottage, and live in comparative peace for the remainder of his days. His daughter, Marianne, is the wife of an unsuccessful shopkeeper, who, it develops during the course of the action, has discounted some notes for a man who has subsequently defaulted. Their daughter, Anna, wishes to marry James Scollard, a bumptious young man whom Muskerry, in order to please Anna, has succeeded in having appointed his successor. The grandfather's life has been one of constant self effacement for his family, and when his daughter asks him to sacrifice his own future comfort in order to save the reputation of the Crillys, he feels justified in his refusal. Finally, however, he agrees to live with them, but their ill treatment drives him to seek refuge in the workhouse of which he had been master. His son in law's unfortunate experience has jeopardized not only his own but likewise Muskerry's savings, so that he is forced to abide in the pauper ward. The sequence of little tragedies culminates in his discovery that, because of his humane management of the institution, he stands in debt to the amount of fifty pounds. The debts incurred by Crilly and the necessity for providing a dowry for Anna have wiped out his savings. Muskerry, weakened and aged by the annoyance to which he has been subjected, dies of an apoplectic stroke at the precise moment that one of his former charges, a blind piper, is set free upon the roads. The bitter satire of the play lies not only in the characterization of the Crillys, the impotent father, the tricky son, the selfish and brutal daughter, and the harassed mother, nor in the striking portrait of the vindictive and cynical porter Felix Tournour, but transfigures the whole situation that makes Thomas Muskerry a village King Lear.

"The Miracle of the Corn" is a little study in symbolism, in which a child of dreams, Aislinn, softens the heart of a dour old farmer in famine time, and when he has exhausted his store of corn in gifts to his neighbors, the bins are miraculously refilled. This one little play is the only evidence in all of his published work of an art that is delicate and fine and minute, an art so exquisite in the embodiment of its conception that the dual illusion of actuality and dream is perfectly sustained, and leaves the reader in doubt as to whether the child Aislinn is a child of reality or the physical expression of the desires of Sheila and her husband. In "The Flute-Player's Story," one of the two little tales of the same volume, there is substantial evidence of his abundant humor. The humor of his plays, however, is more strictly the humor of circumstance as it appears to the observer whose point of view is that of a purely impersonal detachment, it springs rather from the logic of events than from accentuation of character, for to him character is conditioned by the external situation to which it reacts, and from this point of view the consistency of its psychology in his plays is unimpeachable. His humor is bitter and harsh; irony and tragedy are its component elements.

Lord Dunsany, although he has concerned himself little with either the legend or the contemporary life of Ireland, has identified himself with the Celtic literary movement, and is the author of six plays and several volumes of short tales and prose poems. A little volume of "Five Plays," containing "The Gods of the Mountain," "The Golden Doom," "King Argimenes and the Unknown Warrior," "The Glittering Gate" and

"The Lost Silk Hat," appeared in 1914. His
sixth play, "A Night at an Inn," received its first
performance on any stage at the Neighborhood
Playhouse in New York, a theater connected with
the Henry Street Settlement and devoted to the
use of a company of amateur actors and actresses
recruited from the settlement, on April 22nd, 1916.
The predominating quality of Lord Dunsany's
talent lies in the richness of his imagination; he
has created an oriental mythology existing apart
from the limits of time, although the ultimate
struggle is that of man and the gods against ruin-
ing time. With exquisite irony and no little
humor, for he is a master of strongly objectified
situation, he portrays the combat of man with the
gods, the creations of his own ignorance, for the
gods are merely the symbolic expression of man's
lack of control over his experience, and, with time
the destroyer, the illustrations of man's ultimate
futility. The events of his plays, like those of
the tales that he has written, are similar in circumstance to the tales of wonder and of magic in
the Arabian nights. In "King Argimenes" a
captive sovereign finds a sword and by means of
it makes himself again a king; in "The Gods of
the Mountain" seven beggars impersonate the

gods and receive the gifts and the veneration of the people until the gods themselves come down from their mountain and turn the impostors into stone; in "The Golden Doom" a child writes a poem with a golden nugget on the king's great door, and the king, thinking it a prophecy of doom written by the gods, is humbled in his pride, leaving his crown as an offering of appeasement to the deities, whereupon the child takes it away, and the king believes himself saved. In "A Night at an Inn" a band of rogues, led by a decayed aristocrat, have stolen the great ruby from the statue of an Indian god. The priests follow them to an inn in England, but one by one are killed. Finally, when all is thought safe, the rogues are summoned one by one to the garden, where an avenging justice awaits them in the person of the god himself, who wreaks on each a terrible vengeance. "The Glittering Gate" and "The Lost Silk Hat" are little farces, the one telling of the adventures of two dead burglars before the gate of heaven, the other, of a sundered romance and its happy conclusion. Lord Dunsany has contributed to the dramatic literature of the Celtic revival a plenitude of wit and myth-making imagination, and a beautiful prose style poetically cadenced.

The younger playwrights of the Abbey group are, for the most part, realists and students of the contemporary life of the Irish peasantry. Few of them are known on this side of the water except those whose plays appeared in the repertory of the Abbey company on its American tour of 1911–12. The most important in point of dramatic accomplishment have been S. Lennox Robinson, who is at present the producing director of the company, T. C. Murray, St. John G. Ervine, "Rutherford Mayne," "Norreys Connell" (Conal O'Riordan), who succeeded Synge as one of the directors, George Fitzmaurice, Thomas MacDonagh, Seumas O'Kelly and William Boyle. Plays of worth have also been written by Johanna Redmond, by Lewis Purcell, and by Terence J. MacSwiney, although these writers have not been connected with the Abbey.

Lennox Robinson has written five plays: "The Clancy Name" (1908), "The Crossroads" (1909), "Harvest" (1910), "Patriots" (1912) and "The Dreamers" (1915). "The Clancy Name" is a tragic story of the Widow Clancy's shortlived happiness. She has paid off her debts, and is arranging to marry her son to a well dowered girl, when the son confesses to a murder that has puzzled the district. She is horrified, but refuses to let him give himself up to the police, as he wishes, and he, conscience-stricken, throws himself under a passing cart to save a child from being run down by the drunken driver. He is brought to the house, and murmurs incoherently of the murder, which is still in his consciousness, but dies a hero before the neighbors can learn anything that will sully the Clancy name. The excellence of the play is wholly dependent upon the characterization of Mrs. Clancy, the typical resourceful, energetic farmer's wife.

The next three plays in succession are vital drama, each of them carrying a criticism of some phase of Irish life. This faculty for criticism is not limited, however, to this particular author; it seems rather to be a heritage left by Synge to the playwrights that came after him. But whereas Synge's criticism of life is merely incidental, the younger playwrights center their attention upon it, and, while in the plays of Synge it is inherent in either character or plot, in those of the younger group the plot is likely to be somewhat arbitrarily arranged to suit the motives of the critic. With Robinson's plays, however, this is not the case. "The Crossroads" is a study of the new peasant

woman and the old loveless marriage. Ellen Mc-
Carthy is of peasant stock, has gone to Dublin, and
getting a position as servant, has risen to that of
saleslady in a bookshop. In order to give her
sister a chance in Dublin, she returns to the farm,
where she tries to better the conditions of the
rural people by teaching them, through her own
example, methods of scientific agriculture. The
mother marries her off to Tom Dempsey, a brutal,
but rich farmer. She marries him in order to be
able to carry her public-spirited work to a further
degree of efficiency, but he abuses her, and she
rapidly becomes a drudge. Seven years later the
man she loves, now a successful writer, visits her.
Her husband overhears her refusal to go away
with the man, locks her in the room, and goes to
the village to get drunk, promising to make her
"pay for this night's work." She has failed in
her work, in her marriage, and in her life. Her
two children have died, and she herself has lost
all but life. The curtain falls on the husband's
threat. "Harvest" is an indictment of the old
education that prepared the peasant for a position
in town rather than for the rural industry to which
he is fitted. Five children of Timothy Hurley
have been educated in the old way, and at the

expense of the farm and of the life of the one
brother who remains to work it with the father.
All of them are useless in the time of need with
the exception of the one who has been sacrificed,
and continues to be sacrificed, as the play closes,
to the superior education of the others. "Harvest" is a grim little tract, in its problem the dramatic complement of "The Crossroads," a record
of another phase of the most important economic
problem that Ireland is facing today. "Patriots," on the other hand, is a trenchant satire
aimed both at the physical force party, and at the
comfortable agitation of the political leagues that
take their patriotism out in talk. James Nugent,
a political criminal, has been imprisoned for eight-
een years, and returns to find his daughter a
cripple because of his early campaigning, and his
neighbors and friends unwilling to listen to the
talk that made them potential revolutionists after
the Parnell case. He realizes that Ireland is,
after all, a nation of "comfortable shopkeepers,"
as Yeats has said, and that his career has been a
failure and a waste of life. "Patriots" is the
author's best made play in the theatrical sense;
it is more conventional than either "Harvest"
or "The Crossroads," but it marks an advance in

dramatic technique. Like the other two plays, it is a tragedy, and the social criticism of which it is the vehicle is directed toward elements that are firmly rooted in contemporary Irish life. Furthermore, it grips the emotions of its audiences to a far greater extent than either of the other two plays. But time, which made life a tragedy for James Nugent, has disproved Lennox Robinson. The Dublin riots of April, 1916, and the consequent proclamation of martial law throughout Ireland, the capture and arrest of Sir Roger Casement, himself affiliated with the Irish revival, have demonstrated that physical force, taken up by Sinn Fein and the Irish volunteers, is even now a political theory that official Ireland must reckon with.

"The Dreamers" is an historical play, the record of the tragedy of the Emmet uprising of '98; it is effective on the stage, as are all of Robinson's plays, but it is not as important as any of the others. Lennox Robinson is still under thirty; he has written three plays as great in their way as are those of Synge in theirs. Now that Padraic Colum has ceased writing for the theater, he is the most important force among the naturalistic playwrights who are writing in Ireland today. There is

no doubt that Synge was a primary influence upon
his art, just as Granville Barker has been, but
these influences are of little importance in the
consideration of that art as an accomplished product. He too is a regional playwright—it is of the
southwest that he writes—but he is thoroughly
representative of the Ireland of today.

The influence of Synge was the acknowledged
and impelling motive that turned the thoughts of
"Rutherford Mayne" toward the theater. An
actor himself, he has, like Lennox Robinson, experimented and learned his craft in the making of his
plays. He has written four plays, three of them
dealing with the life of County Down, and one
with the peasantry of the Galway bogland. The
chief qualities of his art are the novel beauty and
surging rhythm of his diction, the fidelity of his
plays to the life that he knows, the power of putting before an audience characters that dominate
its consciousness. There is present also in his
dramatic writing a feeling for situation and for
essential drama, although "Rutherford Mayne"
does not write in the vein of the "well-made play,"
but, like Granville Barker, seeks to create an
effect of extreme naturalism and an illusion of life
conceived not in terms of the theater. "The

Drone" (1908) is a comedy telling the story of a
family parasite, a sham inventor of a sham bel-
lows, who saves the day when his brother is
threatened with a suit for breach of promise by a
managing spinster in search of a husband with
money. It portrays with sardonic humor the
avarice of the dour Scotch-Irish farmer, his pride
in his family, his unwillingness to be beaten in a
bargain. "The Turn of the Road" (1906) shows
the tragedy in the life of a stern Puritan father
whose son loves more than all else in life the violin
and its music. The girl that he loves advises him
to give up the life of farmer for that of a musician,
and the father turns him out on the road with his
curse, only realizing later that the city-folk will
never appreciate the boy's wild music, and that he
might have made him a happy man at home.
"The Troth" (1908), is likewise tragedy. A
Protestant and a Catholic peasant agree to lie
in wait for a brutal landlord and kill him, agreeing
that should one be captured, he is to tell nothing
of his accomplice. The landlord is killed, and the
Catholic, who has lost his wife through the landlord's brutality, is captured. But the Protestant
has been the murderer, and the curtain falls as he
faces the horror of his wife. "Red Turf" (1911),

is a tale of a land feud in Galway. The husband of a nagging wife shoots the neighbor and his son who have, by the decision of the law, stolen the land that was her dowry. He does it not because he really wishes to, but because he knows that his wife will never let him forget the grudge, although, at the crucial moment, she is thoroughly frightened and tries to dissuade him.

What little philosophy of life there is in the plays of "Rutherford Mayne" is not conditioned by, nor implicit in the plot itself, but reaches us in the comment of the old men who appear in the plays. The plots themselves are not firmly integrated nor well articulated, but in every instance the characters are powerfully realized, and the plays, in their spare and direct realism, are singularly close to life.

T. C. Murray is a native of County Cork, the locale of his two plays, "Birthright" (1910), and "Maurice Harte" (1912). The first of these is a grim tragedy of the jealousy of two brothers, the elder of whom is the favorite of the parish because of his fine personality and prowess in athletics. The father, in a burst of rage at finding that his son has gone to a feast to celebrate a victory at hurley, disinherits him, and plans to have him emigrate. The younger son, more purely of peasant stock, like the father, is jealous of his brother, who taunts him with having plotted to grab the land. An added motive is his envy of his mother's love for her eldest. In the end he murders his brother, and the curtain falls on the mother's tragedy. It is her portrait, so finely achieved, so universal in its appeal to the emotions, that makes "Birthright," founded on a plot as old as the story of Cain and Abel, a masterpiece of the modern drama.

"Maurice Harte" does for Catholic Ireland just what the plays of "Rutherford Mayne" and St. John Ervine do for Protestant Ireland. Maurice is being educated at Maynooth for the clergy, but after his family have plunged themselves in debt to pay his tuition he discovers that he has no vocation. They persuade him to continue his course in order that his brother may make a successful marriage. He returns to Maynooth, passes with the highest grade at his examination, and is about to be ordained, when the shock of committing this final sacrilege is too much for him, and he loses his reason. The tragedy of her son's madness almost kills the mother, and the family find themselves still in debt, and uncertain whether the marriage can be accomplished after the disgrace has become known.

Patriarchal rule, the tragedy of unrealized family ambitions, the folly that makes the peasantry wish, both for financial and religious reasons, to have their sons become priests; these are the themes employed by T. C. Murray. He is not, like Lennox Robinson, a propagandist, but he is a social critic, although there is no word of criticism in his plays. Their power lies in the grim, unrelieved tragedy of reality; in the direct expression of life as everyone knows it, and since no audience can escape from these plays without sensing this, they constitute the most important social criticism as well as the best dramatic art that the Abbey has brought forth since the days of Synge. T. C. Murray has in two plays attained the highest level reached by the realists; of less accomplishment in quantity than Lennox Robinson, he is of greater in quality.

St. John Greer Ervine is the author of six plays and of two novels. He is a native of Belfast, and the greater part of his work is concerned with the life of the workingmen in that city and in the surrounding country. "Mixed Marriage" (1911), is a study of religious intolerance among the artisans of Belfast. John Rainey, a Protestant, has forgotten his religious prejudice during a strike in which laborers of both faiths are working together to ameliorate their condition and makes speeches advocating the cessation of religious strife. His son Hugh, who is more tolerant, is in love with a Catholic girl, and friendly with the Catholic labor agitator. The father, discovering that Hugh is to marry Nora, drives both away from home, and turns his speeches to denunciation of the Catholics, bringing about a riot, during which Nora is shot by the soldiers. The characterization of the stern, Puritanical father, the sensible and humorous mother, and the lovers is exceedingly well done, and the play is exceptionally successful as a purely objective study of the feelings of Ulster. In the same vein, but slighter in its dramatic material, is "The Orangeman" (1914), which tells how Tom M'Clurg refuses to beat the drum that his father has beaten on every anniversary of the Battle of the Boyne since the first Home Rule Bill was brought in by Gladstone. The father, who is a religious bigot, cannot go to the celebration because of a rheumatic attack, and the son, furious at his bullying, puts his foot through the drum.

"The Magnanimous Lover" (1912), is an excellent acting play in one act the first performance

of which caused a riot in the Abbey akin to that
caused by "The Playboy," Dublin audiences feeling that the word "bastard" was a reflection upon
Irish morality. Maggie Cather has been betrayed
and become the mother of a child by Henry Hinde.
He has left Ireland just before the birth of the
baby, refusing to marry Maggie because she is no
longer a "good woman." Ten years later, having
prospered in Liverpool until it is possible for him
to marry a minister's daughter, he is conscience-
stricken, and although he no longer loves or
respects Maggie, returns to ask her hand in marriage. She, knowing his feelings, refuses to let him
be "saved" from the consequences of his own sin
by marrying her. The play is a splendid study of
life and of emotion, and is exceptionally effective
on the stage. "The Critics" (1913), is a slight
dialogue poking fun at the various Dublin re-
viewers who wrote accounts of the "immorality"
of "The Magnanimous Lover." It is done quite in
the spirit of Molière's little play of criticism, "Le
Critique de l'École des Femmes."

In "Jane Clegg" (1914), the playwright has
turned his attention to England. Henry Clegg is a
weak and irresponsible character, a liar, and has
been unfaithful to his wife. He is hard pressed for

money, for a cause that he does not care to reveal, and she refuses to give him the little she has inherited. He defaults with a check belonging to the firm for which he is a travelling salesman, and when the deficit is discovered appeals to his wife. She pays the debt in order to save the reputation of his children, but discovers that he has used the money to save his mistress, who is about to give birth to a child, and with whom he planned to elope to Canada on the following morning; and tells him to go. And thus he leaves her. As in the other plays, the chief quality upon which "Jane Clegg" depends is the excellence of its characterization. It is, however, from the point of view of dramatic construction, the best of the six plays. The plot is well articulated, and the situations developed forcefully, and as a record of life it is convincingly real and true. In his latest play, "John Ferguson" (1915), St. John Ervine has returned to Ireland and placed his scene in County Down. It relates how the mortgage on John Ferguson's farm is to be foreclosed by Henry Witherow, how Witherow and Jimmy Ceasar each wish to marry Hannah Ferguson and redeem the mortgage, and how Hannah is betrothed to Jimmy, whom she does not love. Then, deciding that she cannot marry him, she goes to Witherow to tell him to foreclose. He wrongs her, and is killed by her brother Andrew, who gives himself up to the police, and then, after all the tragedy, a check arrives from the uncle in America to whom the family had applied for money.

St. John Ervine, like most of the younger group of Irish playwrights, is a realist, interested in the prosaic and matter of fact life that he knows so well, and giving in his plays a careful transcript from it. He has great power of dialogue, and an ambient humor which appears to a greater extent in his novels than in his plays. He is an expert technician, and a creator of characters that seem to possess their own lives, of which his plays but give a glimpse. And in the final analysis, his plays, like those of T. C. Murray, are the product of a close observation and mature reflection about life.

Seumas O'Kelly is a playwright quite in the tradition exemplified by the plays of Robinson, Murray, Mayne, and Ervine. He is the author of two plays, "The Shuiler's Child" (1909), which shows the influence of both Synge and the younger realists, and "The Bribe" (1913), a study of local politics which, like "Patriots," was perhaps influenced by "The Bending of the Bough."

"The Shuiler's Child" exhibits traces of Synge's choice of material in the character of Moll Woods, the "shuiler" or woman of the roads. She has become a vagrant because of a term served in gaol, and her child she has left in the workhouse. There Nannie O'Hea, the wife of a prosperous farmer, and childless, has seen him and adopted him. The Lady Inspector has a quarrel with the foster mother, and recommends that the child be taken away. But the life of Nannie is centered in that of Phil, the child. Moll returns to the workhouse, claims the child, to whom she has a legal right, and returns him to Nannie, realizing that he is not strong enough to endure the life of the roads. As she is leaving Nannie's home, assured of a position on a farm near the child and an opportunity to redeem herself in the eyes of society, she learns that the police have a warrant for her arrest on an old charge. To save the reputation of the child, she gives herself up, knowing that another term in gaol is her final downfall.

"The Bribe" concerns a heavily contested election for the position of dispensary doctor in a small local division. The two young doctors are Luke Diamond, the son of a poor woman who has

spent her little savings on his education, and who
has taken all the honors at college, and Power
O'Connor, the son of the retiring physician, who
is a profligate and degenerate. John Kirwan, the
chairman of the Board of Guardians, has promised to hold aloof at the election, but discovers
that he is hopelessly in debt to the best friend of
O'Connor's father, who is pressing him for immediate payment. He therefore accepts a bribe
from old Doctor O'Connor, and decides the election, against his own conscience, for young O'Connor. Luke Diamond and his mother are ruined,
but although they feel that Kirwan has been
bribed, as they know that other councillors have
been, his reputation for honesty is so great that
they do not dare attack him. Luke therefore
decides to emigrate to Australia. Kirwan's wife
is about to give birth to a child, and Dr. O'Connor
has charge of the case. He is incompetent, however, and things go wrong, and finally, he is forced
to call Luke in to save Mrs. Kirwan. Before
Luke arrives the patient becomes worse, and when
he does arrive, although he is a specialist in such
cases, he can do nothing, and Mrs. Kirwan and the
child die. Such is the retribution allotted to
Kirwan by the dramatist.

O'Kelly's plays both show the social criticism and the pessimism characteristic of the younger Irish dramatists. The criticism in this instance is directed toward the corruption of political life in Ireland, and toward the law, which ruins the life of a woman through no fault of her own. The pessimism in both plays is, like that of Padraic Colum in "Thomas Muskerry," a view of the utter futility of life in the smaller country towns. But the power of the plays is hindered by a tendency toward talkiness that obscures the progress of the action. Unlike T. C. Murray, Seumas O'Kelly does not employ the singularly spare directness of speech which the realistic dramatists find so effective an agent in influencing the emotions of an audience. The underlying ideas of both plays are trenchant and essentially dramatic, but the art of the playwright is deficient in technical ability.

William Boyle has written four plays of life in Galway: "The Building Fund" (1905), "The Eloquent Dempsey" (1906), "Family Failings" (1912) and "The Mineral Workers" (1906). All are in a comic vein, and one at least, "The Building Fund" has been one of the most successful productions made by the Abbey. It tells how a

miserly son and a sly granddaughter are disin-
herited and disappointed by a shrewd old peasant
woman who leaves her fortune and farm to the
building fund of the parish church. The plot is
slight, and the play depends, for its success, upon
a wealth of characterization and capable acting.
The audience, feeling little or no sympathy for
any of the characters, views it in a wholly impersonal mood, and therefore is amused by the
trickiness which results in a certain measure of
tragedy. The other three plays are equally slight
in content and contain little evidence that the
author has attempted a serious interpretation of
Irish life. His plays attain a comfortable medi-
ocrity and some success in the theater, but as a
contribution to dramatic literature they are manifestly unimportant.

"Norreys Connell" (Conal O'Riordan) became
a director of the Abbey in 1909, succeeding J. M.
Synge. He had already contributed a play,
"The Piper" (1908), to the repertory of the company, and he followed it with two others, "Time"
(1909) and "An Imaginary Conversation" (1909).
He has written two other plays, both as yet unproduced, "Shakespeare's End" (1912) and "Rope
Enough" (1914). The first of his plays is a bitter

satire of contemporary Irish political life and feeling thinly veiled under the guise of an incident of the rebellion of '98. It provoked a riot similar to that occasioned by "The Playboy" and "The Magnanimous Lover" at its first performance. In its denunciation of the evils of all the various political parties, of the lack of cohesion obtaining among the various groups of people professedly striving toward the same end, of the lack of efficient action and plenitude of inconsequential oratory, of the fundamental impracticality of the Irish, it contains social criticism of a peculiarly trenchant quality. "Time," a little morality play, and "An Imaginary Conversation," a dialogue between Robert Emmet, Tom Moore, and his sister, are not of great importance. "Shakespeare's End" is likewise slight in conception and in execution. "Rope Enough" is a society comedy of English aristocratic life done in the manner of Wilde, and betraying, in part, the influence of Bernard Shaw and of Granville Barker. It points the rather obvious moral that if a man is given "rope enough" he will surely hang himself. In the fashioning of the dialogue "Norreys Connell" has followed the method, instituted by Granville Barker, of conveying the illusion of real life by reproducing conversation that apparently does not foster the progress of the plot, but merely emphasizes the atmosphere of life. This dialogue, as it is to be found in "Rope Enough" and in the plays of Barker, bears no resemblance to the badly constructed dialogue that mars the art of "The Shuiler's Child"; it involves a difficult process of selection, and is done with deliberate intention, and marks, in its effort to reproduce natural in distinction to dramatic speech, a new theory of the theater.

George Fitzmaurice has written five plays: "The Country Dressmaker" (1907), "The Moonlighter," "The Piedish" (1908), "The Magic Glasses" and "The Dandy Dolls," all of which deal with life in Kerry. Four are comedies, while "The Moonlighter" tells of the tragedy of a rising in the eighties of the last century. "The Piedish" is the brief scene of the death of an old impenitent who hoped to cheat both death and his family by living to finish a piedish that he had been modelling in putty. "The Dandy Dolls" and "The Magic Glasses" both introduce the supernatural and grotesque. But "The Country Dressmaker" is a comedy of actual life, dealing, for the most part, with matchmaking. In this one play alone are the characters strongly realized and the action developed logically. All five plays are marred by a certain verbosity that accomplishes little either in furthering the action or in limning the characters. The dialect in these plays shows the influence of Synge, but it wholly lacks the rhythm and cadence and beauty of color that raised the peasant dialect as Synge employed it to the level of poetic expression.

Johanna Redmond, Lewis Purcell, and Terence MacSwiney have each one play to their credit. Miss Redmond's "Falsely True" (1911) is a lurid little melodrama of the rising of 1803, in which a mother is forced to listen to her son's confession that he has turned informer in order to save his brother. Lewis Purcell's "The Pagan" (1909) is a little comedy of love and elopement in Ulster in the sixth century, not without its satire upon twentieth century Ireland. Terence MacSwiney's "The Revolutionist" (1914) was written with the idea of injecting a little more technical skill into the contemporary Irish drama, and in order to illustrate the claims of the intellectual as against the imaginative drama. It portrays the tragedy of the political reformer who sets his ideals before aught else in the scale of values. The play is well written, the dialogue direct and forceful, and the characters well drawn. To a great degree it is a vehicle for the social criticism of its author. An earlier tragedy having political reform as its subject is "When the Dawn Is Come," by the late Thomas MacDonagh, one of the younger generation of poets and critics, which was produced at the Abbey in 1908. It deals with the revolution in Ireland in the coming days, and shows the tragedy that befell the leader because he dealt with the enemy in a fashion that resembled treason, but which effectually won his cause. In plot, the play is identical with Verhaeren's "Les Aubes" which the author had never read. It is written in poetic prose, but fails to attain true dramatic speech. Because of its patriotic qualities it scored some success. It seems, however, that the play was not without some prophecy of truth. As the present lines are being written [1] news has come to America telling of the capitulation of the Provisional Government of the Republic of Ireland. One of the Commissioners of that government, and a leader in the revolt, was Thomas MacDonagh.

[1] May 1st, 1916. See the "New York Times" for text of the Proclamation, published in the issue of that date.

Joseph Campbell (Seosamh MacCathmhaoil) known also as an illustrator and the writer of some very beautiful poems and prose sketches of life in Donegal, has written one play. "Judgment" (1912) is a record of life in Donegal, a play which, in its grim tragedy and wild beauty is reminiscent of Synge. It concerns Peg Straw, a demented old wanderer who has been turned away from the house of a peasant woman expecting the birth of her first child. The action takes place in the house from which she has been turned away. She is beaten by the tinkers a little way from the house, and the audience hears the cries of her suffering. Finally she returns to die in the cabin, so thoroughly frightening the wife that her child is born prematurely. During the wake held for Peg a stranger enters the house, bringing with him the atmosphere of the wild night on the roads outside. He quarrels with all there, and finally, as an old man is telling that Peg had lost her mind because she had murdered her baby, the stranger proclaims himself the child whom she had thought to drown, and is turned out of the house in which his mother lies dead and unburied. The quality of this play is as instinctively poetic as that of "Riders to the Sea"; it possesses the same sense of remoteness from the ordinary life that we know, the same tragic fate produced by the circumstances of a wild and primitive life, the same beauty of speech and heightened imagination as characteristic of the people who live that life.

The dramatic movement in Ireland has undergone a curious change during the sixteen years that have elapsed since its inception. It began as an attempt to produce literary plays; it brought forth poetic tragedy, "intellectual" drama, and realistic satire of contemporary life. Then, with Yeats as the dominating spirit, it was hoped that a school of writers having at their command the resources of a beautiful language, would arise and create a folk-drama, and poetic plays founded upon legendary lore. With the coming of J. M. Synge the dominant influence suffered a change. Realism took the place of romance; the wild, primitive, elemental nature of the peasant became the chief interest, and the peasant conceived in terms of spirituality and mystical belief and living wholly in a world of dreams, was lost sight of in the ensuing reaction against the theories of Yeats. In the plays of Synge the romantic and the realistic conceptions of life met in their fullest development. They influenced the subsequent work of Yeats himself,

bringing him to deal less and less with the world of
the imagination, unburdening his work of its
"dream-drenched will," and bringing it into closer
touch with life. What they have done for the
younger generation of playwrights is obvious to the
reader acquainted with the work of Robinson,
Murray, Mayne, and even that of Padraic Colum.
The newer playwrights have concentrated their
attention upon the life of today, whether that of
the peasantry, the townsmen or the official classes.
The tradition of "Celticism" has almost wholly
disappeared from contemporary Irish drama. It
may be questioned whether the fate-burdened
tragic peasant of the plays of today is more truthful to the life of Ireland as it is actually being lived
than was the "stage Irishman" of Boucicault and
his school, or the visionary dreamer of the earlier
work of Yeats and of A. E. Almost the only followers of Yeats of any importance have been Lady
Gregory, whose historical plays are not especially
valuable as literature, nor especially powerful as
drama, and William Sharp, whose plays remain
unproduced. The younger school refuses to find
consolation and refuge either in its dreams or in an
heroic past. They are concerned with the problems of today in an effort to influence the life of to-

morrow. They produce social criticism in order to enforce the changes which they desire Ireland to undergo; if they are extreme in their satire and pessimistic in their tragic conception of life, it is because propaganda must necessarily enforce its point by exaggerating and emphasizing conditions. Their propaganda, however, is not one of art, but of actual experience. What these newer playwrights have done is to turn from art to life, and by doing so they have laid the foundations of their art upon a firmer soil.

In expression the newer dramatists have followed the innovation begun by Dr. Hyde, continued by Lady Gregory, and for the first time employed in the drama by J. M. Synge. In doing so they have fulfilled at least one of the visions of Yeats, who above all desired a folk-theater. The Abbey is essentially a folk-theater in that the greater number of plays produced there deal with the life of the peasantry. Folk-imagination and folk-poetry are qualities inherent in many of these plays, only, however, when they are implicit in the essential drama, and never gratuitiously applied, as they threatened to become in the work of Yeats.

The acting of the Abbey company is marked by the same simplicity of expression, the same econ-

omy of means, the same dignity of feeling as that
which characterizes the plays which they enact.
There is very little "stage-business" in the commonly accepted theatrical sense of the phrase.
The actors and actresses have studied peasant life
thoroughly, and they recreate it with exact and
painstaking realism. Their chief reliance is laid
upon beauty and expression in diction, and they
have learned from the French theater how it is
possible to convey character in voice, gesture, and
appearance, with the minimum of action. Productions at the Abbey are also exceptionally simple,
although in the case of the poetic drama an attempt has been made to convey the atmosphere
and mood of the play by means of the new methods of suggestive stagecraft. It must be remembered that these results in acting, producing, and
even in the character of the plays themselves have
been as greatly enforced by external conditions as
they have been consciously sought for. The Abbey itself is a small theater; the company that
originally occupied it was composed chiefly of men
and women without previous stage experience, and
the training in acting that they have had has led
them in an opposite direction from the professional stage as it has been in England and in the

United States. But the Abbey has had a great deal of influence, not only in Ireland and in England, but in the United States, where the recent creation of "little theaters" has been principally encouraged by its example.

Its greatest importance lies in the fact that it has given artistic expression to the race consciousness, and that it has been productive of a new and powerful dramatic literature. For the Abbey playwrights are doing the most noteworthy work that is being done for the English speaking stage today.

CHAPTER V

THE NOVEL, FOLK-LORE, AND OTHER PROSE

THE novel has been the one literary form in the manipulation of which Irish writers have been conspicuously deficient. The plays of Synge are sufficiently great in dramatic achievement to bear comparison with the work of any of the contemporary Continental dramatists; the dramatic poems of William Butler Yeats are nearly if not quite the equals of those of Maeterlinck, and his lyric verse and the poetry of A. E. is of as high an order as that written anywhere in the last twenty-five years. But if we look for a single Irish novelist the quality of whose work assures him of a parity of stature with any of these, the search is likely to end in failure. This is all the more remarkable since, at the outset of the Romantic Revival, it was an Irish novelist, Maria Edgeworth, who taught English writers to find a social as well as an artistic interest in peasant life, and who first brought the humanitarian motive, destined in the Victorian period to occupy the chief attention of English writers, into English fiction. A little later the works of Charles Lever, of Samuel Lover, and of William Carleton attained popularity, though none of the three were essentially significant authors. Carleton, who knew Gaelic, might possibly have inaugurated an earlier renascence of interest in the Irish, had he not been too covetous of popularity, and written of Ireland purely for English readers during the greater part of his career. From the time of Carleton until the late eighties of the last century no Irish novelist of even passing note appeared upon the horizon.

It was in 1886 that George Moore published "A Drama in Muslin," following it in the next year with "Parnell and his Island." He had spent his boyhood at Moore Hall, the family estate in Mayo, which, upon the death of his father, he inherited. It is his own confession that Ireland had little appeal for him in his youth, and, after studying at Oscott College, he went to London to learn the art of painting. At twenty-one he migrated to Paris, enrolling at the Academie Julian, but soon discovered that painting was not his art. He wrote a little volume of erotic verse which unfortunately has disappeared from public view. Just as he had come in contact with most important movements in English art while studying in London, and had known Whistler and the Pre-raphaelites, so in Paris he came to know intimately the artists who were soon to become famous as the Impressionist school. This acquaintance, and Moore's own study of art enabled him, in 1893, to write "Modern Painting" which, although the verdict of time has in some instances not borne out his judgment, was the first adequate discussion of the esthetics of modern art to be written in England. After ten years of life in Paris, reverses in fortune compelled him to return to England, where he began his career as a writer. In 1883 he wrote "A Modern Lover," and in the following year, "A Mummer's Wife." Then came the two books first mentioned, and in rapid succession "Spring Days," "Impressions and Opinions," a volume of criticism published in 1891, "Modern Painting," his two early experiments with the drama, "The Strike at Arlingford" (1893) and "Journeys End in Lovers Meeting" (1894), and "Esther Waters," published in 1894.

In 1898, with the publication of "Evelyn Innes," he had evidenced an interest in the Irish revival, which, with the outbreak of the Boer War, sent him to Ireland in 1899, where he remained for

eleven years. During his residence there he wrote
the plays which have been discussed in another
chapter, and seven books. These were "Sister
Teresa," a sequel to "Evelyn Innes," published in
1901; "The Untilled Field," a collection of stories
of varying length, in 1903; "The Lake" in 1905,
"Memoirs of My Dead Life" in 1906; and three
volumes of "Hail and Farewell" "Ave," (1911),
"Salve" (1912) and "Vale" (1914), the first of
which was published in 1911 just after his departure from Dublin. The Celtic episode of his
career closed with the publication of "Hail and
Farewell," and he has returned to life in London.

The foundations of his art were laid during his
ten years of residence in Paris; it is usually unprofitable to trace literary influences, but in the
case of George Moore the influences are so thoroughly patent that they seem to form the basis of
his art. Above all others, if we wish to arrive at
the fundamental experiences out of which he
writes, we must place his own life. That it has
been full and varied, that his contact has been
wide and his appreciations versatile beyond that
of any other contemporary author must be evident
to every reader of his novels. In Paris he served
his apprenticeship to all the arts; he returned to

London a critic possessing a background of culture
that was anything but superficial, a cosmopolitan
in his interests, a novelist who had modelled his
conception of his art upon that of Zola.

He is rarely a subjective realist, and although he
has analysed himself frequently in his writing, the
analysis in each case is as clearly objective as is
that of the characters between whose temperament
and his there exists the widest possible divergence.
Apart from this, his art is almost entirely impersonal; almost, but not quite entirely, for the re-
curring theme of revolt against the conventionally
accepted code of morality is an expression of one
of the dominant motives of his view of life.   But
if he has not unduly obtruded his own personality
in his art, he has at least revealed therein his
interests, and the personalities of those people who
have attracted him most among his acquaintances.
"Hail and Farewell" is the example that most
readily comes to mind, but there are others.   In
the first version of "Evelyn Innes," the character
of Ulick Dean is clearly a portrait of Yeats, and in
the second version, the portrait is a composite of
Yeats and of A. E.   In the same novel Mr. Innes is
Arnold Dolmetsch, and for the characters of Mgr.
Mostyn and of Sir Owen Asher, the author drew

upon certain of the qualities of mind of Edward
Martyn and of himself.   Dick Lennox, in "A
Mummer's Wife," is, as the author tells us, a
portrait of Dick Maitland, an acquaintance of the
seventies in London, while Esther Waters was
modelled upon his charwoman in Victoria Street,
and Ralph Ellis, about whom we hear in "The
Lake" may be traced to Edouard Dujardin, the
author of "La Source du Fleuve chretien."   The
author's own interests appear to a very great extent either as a background to the essential story,
or in intercalary sections.   The background of
"Evelyn Innes" is fullest in this respect; music,
religion, painting, literature are drawn upon in its
composition.   In "The Lake" there is again the
background of a religious problem, and some excellent criticism of art appears in the letters of
Rose Leicester.   It would be futile to point out
these various correspondences between the author's work and his personal experiences and
temperament except for the purpose of illustrating
his underlying methods as an artist.   He has observed life very carefully and analysed character
thoroughly; he has explored many intellectual
paths, and, finally, he has always been sensitive to
all emotional and sensuous experience.   And from

this eclecticism he has woven the tissue of his art.

The outstanding quality of his writing, and the one wherein he excels any other contemporary English novelist, is his ability to project his characters into life, and to create for each of them a complete psychology. There is, throughout the whole course of Moore's writing, not a single "stock character" to be found, not even a single character of which we can say that he is true to "type." Each of the personages that find their way into his novels is sharply and clearly drawn as an individual, reacting to life in exactly the fashion that we should expect them to from our knowledge of their past experience. And since the author has chosen to tell his story by revealing the reaction of every character concerned therein, this quality of inevitability in their psychological composition is the foundation of their truth to reality. The professed naturalist in art follows a method similar to that of the scientist; he collects innumerable facts from which he makes a selection, and the generalization that he draws from the results of this process is a complete description of a single phase of life. This was the method of Zola, and in the main it has been the method of George Moore.

The naturalist usually achieves a description of life that is no more vital or dynamic than a scientific formula; it bears the same relation to life that the formula for the composition of water bears to the chemical process from which water results. It is usually a description of life, it tells facts about life, but it does not set life before you. And it is in this quality of setting life before the reader, of giving him an "imitation" of life by imitating the methods of nature, that George Moore has excelled.

The other great quality of his writing lies in what may be termed the art of the background. Here Moore the novelist profits, in many instances, by the experiences of Moore the critic of the arts. In "Evelyn Innes" the reader's senses are wooed by the many beautiful passages descriptive of the effect of music, by the sensuous impressions of Evelyn's room with its delicate eighteenth century furniture and exquisite Boucher drawings; by the description of a room, in this case the motivating cause in the story, in "The Lovers of Orelay." In "The Mummer's Wife" and "Esther Waters," two stories in which the background is one of almost unrelieved sordidness, his genius for conveying concrete impression is even more apparent. And in "The Lake," where the background of the lonely, beautiful, wistful Irish landscape is the spring of all action, it is directed toward an essential symbolism.

George Moore, rather than any other writer, has been the playboy of recent English literature. Early in his career he voiced the rebellion against traditional morality that has become one of the chief concerns of his art; and his French training led him to a somewhat freer expression of sex than that to which modern English literature has been accustomed. One cannot quarrel with an artist concerning his choice of subject, for criticism is only occupied with the results achieved, and these results must be measured, in the case of a writer, by the effect upon his readers. For a man to claim as Moore does, that Christianity has lowered the status of woman, and has founded its morality upon the principle that sexual intercourse is unobjectionable when licensed by a ceremony, but reprehensible otherwise, is for him merely to express an opinion. In his opinion the sexual function is as truly an expression of the creative impulse as in the creation of a work of art. And in this he is merely following the doctrine of Plato. But the difference between Plato and George

Moore lies in a difference in the emotional reaction of the reader. The one dilates the emotions; the other degrades them. Moore's greatest defect as a writer lies in his preoccupation with sex. It is a defect that is especially glaring in a professed naturalist in art, for life does not entirely resolve itself into sensualism, and Moore, in subordinating all experience to the exercise of a single function, betrays a limited and impoverished perspective on life. In this respect, and it is a defect that mars almost one half of his work, Moore, like his compatriots, Wilde and Shaw, consciously attempted to shock the English public, and succeeded. When he came to Ireland, he forsook the Catholic for the Protestant faith; but although he published "The Lake" (1905) and "The Untilled Field" (1903) during his residence there, he was not excoriated, as was Yeats upon the first performance of "The Countess Cathleen," by the Irish clergy; and this must have proved a bitter disappointment.

Of his purely Irish writing, the two early books, "A Drama in Muslin" (1886) and "Parnell and his Island" (1887) may be briefly passed over. "A Drama in Muslin" is powerfully written in Moore's earlier and more realistic manner; and since it is concerned with an Ireland that has disappeared

with the enforcement of the Land Acts, its chief
value today is as a record of the feudal, landlord-
ridden Ireland of two generations ago. "Parnell
and his Island" is a collection of sketches, satiric in
their vein, written about Ireland from an English
point of view. "Evelyn Innes," as has been
intimated, touched briefly upon modern Ireland
and the literary movement in the character of
Ulick Dean, who is concerned with folk-lore,
ancestral memory, and pyschic research in the
manner of Yeats and of A. E. "The Untilled
Field" was begun as a series of stories to be translated into Gaelic by Taidgh O'Donoghue with the
purpose of serving as good modern literature for
the students of the Gaelic League. It is written
sparely and with a barrenness of style unlike
Moore's other work, possibly because it was
merely to serve the translator's purposes. But the
stories themselves go to the heart of Irish character and illustrate the fine qualities of Moore's
realism in their handling of Irish peasant life. In
the character of Father MacTurnan, the author
has portrayed with wonderful fidelity the temperament of the gentle, superstitious old priest between
whose psychology and his own there could be no
wider divergence. This study of celibate tempera-

ment, foreshadowed in the three stories of an earlier period in his career, "Celibates," proves the fundamental impersonality of his art.

"The Lake" many critics believe to be the best writing of the author's "later manner." It is, needless to say, beautifully written, and is the one novel of his later years which expresses the effect of the Celtic episode in his career upon his art. There is a certain gentle beauty and a certain wistfulness and pathos of emotional content in the writing of it that did not appear in any of the author's work until he had come to reside in Ireland. But whether his own vision of the dun west of Ireland is responsible, or whether he read into the landscape much that he felt in the poetry of Yeats and saw in the paintings of A. E. cannot be determined. Certain it is that the rippling, gleaming hardness of his earlier style, a Celtic characteristic apparent in the writing of Wilde and of Shaw, was softened and made sensitive to a beauty that he had not felt before. "Memoirs of my Dead Life" contains only one impression of Ireland; in "Resurgam," descriptive of his mother's funeral, he expresses the wish to be buried with his fathers in the cemetery of Lough Gara.

"Hail and Farewell" is a delightfully amusing

record of his connection with the Irish revival, and an account of his residence in Dublin. It is quite unreliable as to fact, but it contains some malicious and roguish criticism of the men who were writing in Ireland while he lived there. "Euphorian in Texas" published in the " English Review " for July, 1914, is an omitted chapter of that work, a *chronique scandaleuse* in the manner of "The Lovers of Orelay."

Moore's effect upon the Celtic revival in literature has been slight, although he has influenced some of the younger realistic novelists. Fundamentally opposed to the spirit of the movement, he entered it confessedly out of curiosity, was influenced in turn by Yeats, Martyn, Eglinton, and chiefly by A. E., and left it because he felt that Ireland, after all, was not his natural environment.

To that period of the renascence belongs the work of William Buckley, Shan Bullock, and "George Birmingham" (Rev. J. O. Hannay). William Buckley is a writer known by one volume, "Croppies Lie Down" (1903), a realistic story of life in Ulster; since writing which he has done nothing of any great importance. Shan Bullock writes of the lives of the farmers in the northwest. Also a realist, he deals after the manner of Thomas Hardy in the "Wessex Tales" with the bitter, unrelenting hardship of wreaking a bare existence in the Orange counties of the north. "George Birmingham" is a Protestant clergyman of Westport, whose "Spanish Gold," "The Seething Pot" (1904) and "General John Regan" (1913) are all, in their way, excellent studies of life in the west. He was the first novelist to treat Irish life with something of the humor that Lady Gregory has in her plays. The Hon. Emily Lawless has also written of the west coast and of the legend connected therewith. Canon Sheehan has written several pleasantly humorous novels, of which "My New Curate" (1899) is the best; he and the two ladies who employ the double pseudonym of " E. OE. Sommerville and Martin Ross" belong to a generation of writers which has almost disappeared since the beginning of the renascence. William Butler Yeats, during his London period, experimented with the novel, and produced "John Sherman" (1891), a tale of Mayo and London, and "Dhoya" (1891) a tale of ancient Ireland, neither of which is fundamentally important.

The renascence has, however, brought forth two novelists who stand in the front rank of contemporary English writing, and whose work, unlike that of George Moore, is the direct product of the literary movement in Ireland. They are St. John G. Ervine and James Stephens.

Ervine, whose plays have been discussed in a previous chapter, is the author of a novel of life in Belfast, "Mrs. Martin's Man" (1915), a volume of miscellaneous sketches, "Eight O'Clock and Other Studies" (1915), and a novel of London, "Alice and a Family" (1915). Like Padraic Colum, he is concerned in his plays, and also in his novels, with the great middle class which he considers the arteries of the race, and which lives, whether in town or country, a life characteristically its own. His approach to life is singularly direct, and his interest lies rather in the mental life of his characters in its relation to their social life than in the purely external details of existence. The tragedy of physical hunger in the peasant life of Ireland is largely a thing of the past, and has been replaced by a spiritual bankruptcy and a reoccupation with the means rather than with the end of life that is reflected in the work of men like Ervine and Bullock. In "Mrs. Martin's Man" he has written the tragedy of a woman whose existence was a career of altruism. Her history is that of a life baulked in its emotional and intellectual pos-

sibilities, a victory for the force of circumstance
that all but destroyed her, were it not for the fund
of common sense with which she opposed fate.
Her humor is homely and shrewd, and like that
of Alice, the little cockney girl in his novel of
London, it comes of direct contact with experience. Ervine treats life simply and impartially,
with a degree of impersonalism that is reminiscent
of Tourgenieff; he conceives it as a continuous
process, without beginning and without end, and,
in making the selection that art demands, he
chooses only a point of departure and one of conclusion. He obtrudes no moral conviction upon
his audience, but, as he has said in a critical essay [1]
the rebuke lies in the material of his art and in the
motivation of life as he sees it being lived by the
people of whom he writes. The fine qualities of
his work are the strongly conceived and perfectly
realized characterization, the completeness of his
vision of life, and his genuine dramatic instinct.
His "Eight O'clock and Other Studies" contain
in a brief compass some of the most dramatically
powerful writing that has been done by any of the
authors connected with the Irish movement, and

[1] "The Irish Dramatist and the Irish People," " Forum,"
June, 1914.

make evident the reason for St. John Ervine's
success as a novelist.   His fundamentally dramatic conception of life as he treats it in the novel
may perhaps be due to the fact that his training
was that of the playwright; to whatever influence
it is due, however, his work marks an advance upon
any of the prose fiction written by contemporary
Irish authors of the realistic school.

The work of James Stephens would seem, at
first sight, to be as widely removed in content and
spirit from the novels of St. John Ervine as it is in
expression.   But this disjunction is only apparent,
and the distinction is hardly as real as it looks to
be.   James Stephens began his literary career as a
poet and he has continued writing verse, although
his greatest success has been gained as a novelist.
A little of the legend of his early life is told by
George Moore in "Vale"; he is reputed to have
tramped the length and breadth of Ireland, to
have been adopted by an applewoman in Belfast,
but whether there is merely one of the myths of
which Dublin so often makes the authors of the
renascence heroes, or an exaggeration of Moore's,
is difficult to say.   Certain it is that his discovery
as a writer was due to A. E.

The fundamental point of view that underlies his

approach to life consists in regarding everything that forms a part of human experience as a part of reality. Understanding of life is achieved only in the degree that life is experienced, and the sole open sesame to existence lies in keenness of perception and sensitiveness of intuition. To live adequately is to realize, emotionally and intellectually, the widest range of experience that life offers to the individual, and to hold the spirit open to the dynamic force of change.

Society he sees as a highly sophisticated organization, largely built upon settled convictions, time-savers in thinking, the purpose of which is the definition and limitation of the liberties of the individual. The conduct of life, for him, is a product of the interpretation of experience by the individual; conviction is a confession of a limited knowledge of life, and since life appears to have the character of a flux, an inadequate reflection of experience. Truth for him, as for William James, is the good in the way of belief; a conception is true if it entails a practically useful result intellectually or spiritually. It is a quality that adheres not to life itself, but to a human interpretation of it. The good presents itself to him as those factors of experience which have been comprehended and conquered, and which may be counted upon as invariably in result under similar conditions. The factors which have eluded conquest are called false; wrong is a quality to be predicated of the unsolved problems of experience. Things which have been true become false, and new conceptions arise to take their place, and a similar progress is true of the spiritual life. And James Stephens, accepting experience as the criterion of verifiability of any hypothesis, brings down to earth the gods as they live now, and leaves unrealized the divine unity which he believes in the process of generation as the course of progress advances. For humanity is constantly making more God just as it is constantly making more truth.

The author of "Euphues" was the first English novelist to bring the novel indoors, and to give us a picture of social life and manners as they were developed by an age that for the first time in history began to possess that privacy of existence which we deem so necessary today. The essential contribution of James Stephens to the trend of modern fiction lies in the fact that unlike Lyly, he has taken the novel from the narrow confines of the house and brought it again into the open

air. In the degree that his interest is confined
to the novelty in the unchartered corners of experience, he is a romanticist; but the romantic
for him is always identified with the natural and
real, for he has taken the modern mind and freed
it from the trammels imposed by civilization,
and given it birth in a more natural form of life.
Romance he finds in what to nature would have
been the commonplace had not society intervened, and by making nature unnatural, made
natural life romantic in its splendid isolation. So
that the people in his novels, although they possess the modern mind, live in an amoral world and
deal directly with experience.

"Humor," says the angel Finaun in "The
Demigods," "is the health of the mind." Humor
consists for him in preserving an attitude of
openmindedness, in a sensitive awareness to the
quality of life, in the denial of completed and un-
changeable conviction. Humor, viewing the human will baffled by a wall of circumstance that it
can neither evade nor penetrate, conceives the
situation not as tragedy, but as irony, and that,
in the novels of James Stephens, is the attitude
of the gods. The eternal combat between good
and evil resolves itself into the struggle of man to

achieve ever more complete control over experience, and failure in the contest being ironic, is
more tragic than tragedy itself, in that it is comprehended from the vantage of humor.

"Literature," he has said in a recent essay,[1]
"is something more than art; it is the expression
of philosophy in art, and is at once the portrayal
of an individual and a racial psychology. A
writer is not one who portrays life; he is one who
digests life, and every book of his is a lecture on
the state of his mental health." The quality most
commonly ascribed to the art of James Stephens
is that of imagination, and this perhaps more than
any other quality of his art, will illustrate that he
is essentially a realist. The basis of imagination
in art is a close observation of life and a profound
insight into character and motive. The language
of imagination is essentially that of a mind sensitive to the varied impressions that life registers
upon the individual consciousness; expression, far
from being a product of remoteness from life, is
enriched only in so far as it depends upon experience for introspection alone will produce but an
arid vocabulary. The artist, therefore, can find

[1] "The Old Woman's Money," "Century Magazine,"
May, 1915.

his imagination only in training his observation, in the cultivation of life itself, for immediate experience is the foundation of all true art. It is precisely this that James Stephens has done: "The Crock of Gold" (1910), "Here Are Ladies" (1913), "The Charwoman's Daughter" (1912), or, as it is called in the American edition, "Mary, Mary," and "The Demigods" (1914) are the fruit of experience and reflection upon it.

His chief, and perhaps his only, interest is humanity. He can be gentle, protesting, vigorous, and in full rebellion against modern life, but his work is leavened always by a rich humor that is new to literature. "The Crock of Gold" (1910), the best piece of imaginative writing that has been done in English letters in many years, is a book so varied in its temper, so merry and so sane in its fundamental contentions, so baffling in its spirit that comment would be impertinent if possible at all. "The Charwoman's Daughter" (1912) is the first novel of Dublin life today that has been written; it is also a remarkably tender picture of the unfolding of a girl's mind. "Here Are Ladies" (1913) is as bitterly ironic, in part, as is his poetry, and contains some exceptionally powerful studies of character. "The Demigods"

(1914), his last novel, continues the vein of "The Crock of Gold."

Stephens and Ervine are the two outstanding novelists of contemporary Ireland whose work directly reflects the influence of the literary movement. There remains one other writer, who if he has not attained equally as an artist, has done work of distinction. Patrick MacGill has written two sequential novels, "Children of the Dead End" (1914) and "The Rat Pit" (1915), dealing with one of the most important social and economic problems that the thinkers in Ireland are facing; peasant poverty, and its consequence, migratory and casual labor. Both novels are, in a sense, autobiographical. The first deals with the life of a peasant lad, come of an impoverished family of fisher-folk in Donegal, whose services are auctioned off in the labor market and who later becomes one of the bands of migratory laborers who cross to Scotland each summer as harvest hands. The second deals with the girl that he loves, who is wronged by the son of the farmer to whom she hires out, and who finally becomes a woman of the streets, only to die in the utmost squalor in Glasgow. The two together present a picture of the misery of peasant life in one part of

Ireland and of the greater misery to which the peasants sometimes escape in the underworld of the cities that is not easily forgotten. Patrick MacGill has attempted to rouse the social conscience of Ireland and of England in somewhat the same way and to somewhat the same conditions that the I. A. O. S. has done. His books come out of the warp and woof of life, and in their telling are so relentlessly natural, and exhibit so curious a lack of rhetorical indignation, that their power as social documents can be compared to that of "Crime and Punishment." The same dispassionate presentation of fact marks the work of MacGill and of the Russians; perhaps, indeed, because back of both Irish and of Russian literature there is a social consciousness seeking expression, and revolting against the traditional acceptance of existing conditions.

In the field of folk-lore much important work has been done that in a measure provided the foundations upon which the earlier writers of the renascence built. The work of Dr. P. W. Joyce ("Old Celtic Romances," 1879), of Standish O'Grady ("Heroic Period," 1878; "Cuchulain and his Contemporaries," 1880), of Dr. Hyde and of Dr. Sigerson has already been commented upon.

William Larminie for a while devoted some attention to the collection of lore, and published a volume of "West Irish Folk-Tales" (1895), Violet Russell, the wife of A. E., produced "Children of the Dawn" (1914), Lady Gregory wrote "Cuchulain of Muirthemne" (1903), "The Kiltartan History Book" (1909), "Gods and Fighting Men" (1904) and William Butler Yeats gave us "Stories of Red Hanrahan" (1904) and "The Celtic Twilight" (1893).

All this work has been important, chiefly because it provided the material upon which the writers of the renascence were to found a great part of their art, and in two instances at least, it has in itself been great literature. These two are the work of Lady Gregory and of Yeats. Mrs. Russell's "Children of the Dawn" is a retelling of the cycle of the Fianna in very simple and very beautiful English, written with so evident a poetic feeling that it holds the interest of both children and their elders. Patriotic Americans will find it profitable to compare the work of this Irish authoress with the beautiful volume of "Tales of the Enchanted Islands of the Atlantic" by Thomas Wentworth Higginson; that it does not suffer by comparison with the work of the gentle and lamented Bostonian illustrates the high quality of Mrs. Russell's art.

Lady Gregory was inspired to an interest in the collection of folk-lore by William Butler Yeats, and she, in turn inspired him with the idea of re-writing many of his "Tales of Red Hanrahan" in folk-idiom. Her "Gods and Fighting Men" is a work of enduring value, but her fame as an inter-preter of legend is likely to rest upon "Cuchulain of Muirthemne," which is more ambitious in its scope than the later book, or than "A Book of Saints and Wonders." What she has done is to select from among many versions of the folk-tales of the Cuchulain cycle those which best fit into a con-nected whole, rejecting an episode here and adding one from another version in its place, interpreting in another place a passage so remote from modern feeling as to be almost incomprehensible to us, and thus achieving a retelling of the legends that will bear the same relation to us as audience as did the original versions to their audiences. Finally, she has clothed the legends in the dialect of Kiltartan, both because she is a subscriber to the "language theory" and because the idiom is well suited to an effort that in its original intention was oratorical rather than literary. Lady Gregory has not scrupled to acknowledge her debt to many of the modern folk-lorists of more literal tendencies, among them O'Grady and Professor Kuno Meyer, the brilliant German philologist who has done so much for the Irish renascence in this field and for the Gaelic League.   The Irish legends are usually too greatly supernatural in their texture to appeal to the modern mind to as great an extent as do the Greek or Scandinavian.   There is seldom to be found any motivation arising from purely human interests or psychology, although they are expressive of a very beautiful chivalric standard of life, of a certain mysticism in dealing with the world of nature, and in one instance at least, in the tale of Deirdre, have given us one of the most pathetic stories in the world's literature.   It is, however, in their conception of the vitalism of nature that they are most interesting to us, since this conception is basic in the work of many of the modern poets. And Lady Gregory's translations are remarkable for the fidelity and beauty with which she has rendered this old feeling of the hidden presence of nature in its many moods.

William Butler Yeats has concerned himself less with the heroic legend, in his prose writing, than he has with the folk-tales that he has heard in his journeys over the country. The "Stories of Red Hanrahan," written in the Kiltartan idiom, and dealing with the life of a hedge-schoolmaster and the legend that grew up about him after his death he has written simply and with directness; in "The Secret Rose" (1897), in the same volume, he has recorded visions of the fairies of contemporary rural Ireland, and of the heroic past, and in "The Celtic Twilight" he has given us the most beautiful of all his prose writing in "Dust Hath Closed Helen's Eye," a tale of the blind poet Raftery and of the lovely Mary Hynes, whom he loved and for whom he died. This interest in folk-tale and in fairy lore and a growing interest in symbolism and mystic philosophy led him to write "Rosa Alchemica" (1897) and "The Tables of the Law" (1904) neither of which are as successful as artistic creations as are his prose tales.

Of late years folk-lore has interested the purely literary artists of the renascence rather less than it did originally at the inception of the movement. With the coming of writers who found their material in the changing social conditions of peasant life, and who look to the future rather than to the past as a refuge from the present, the world of imagination and legend has practically disappeared from contemporary Irish writing. Therefore the interest in folk-tale and poetry, and much of the writing that came of that interest is of greater importance as an influence upon creative writing, and as an indication of the earliest direction taken by that writing, than as a literary product in itself of enduring importance.

This influence is exemplified at the height of its power in the writings contributed to the literature of the renascence by William Sharp under the pseudonym of "Fiona Macleod." During the eleven years that elapsed between the publication of "Pharais" in 1894 and the death of the author in 1905, "Fiona" was certainly the most widely known and talked of author of the Celtic group. For this two reasons may be advanced; the widespread interest in "her" writings was caused in part by the mystery with which "she" surrounded "herself," and in part by the qualities of style that are present in the writings themselves. A year after the death of Sharp the secret was revealed, a secret which many had guessed but which had always been denied, and in 1912 Mrs. Sharp officially acknowledged it in her memoir of her husband. Mrs. Sharp has recorded her belief in the theory of dual personality which Sharp himself

thought responsible for his writings as "Fiona," a
brief comment upon which has been made else-
where in the course of this study, and the problem
has some interest for psychologists. Sharp had,
however, been given to the perpetration of literary
hoaxes, and the quality of his writings as Fiona
precluded the use of his own name, familiar as that
name was to readers as that of a critic and novelist, so that there seems little necessity to believe
that the consciousness of another self was immediately responsible for his Celtic writing. Although a Scotchman by birth and a Londoner in
his mature life, his work as "Fiona Macleod"
belongs to the Irish renascence of letters, having
been directly influenced by it, and, in the case of
his plays, having been written especially for it.

He does not enter into the previous discussion of
the drama chiefly because his two plays, "The
Immortal Hour" (1900) and "The House of
Usna" (1900), although written for "The Irish
Literary Theatre" were never produced by it, and
because his work as a dramatist is not of any compelling importance. The publication of his critical
essay, "Celtic," wherein he recorded his disbelief
in the separatist political movement, and his belief
that Ireland's destiny of greatness was to be ful-

filled in the absorption of the race by other races, a belief to which he had given voice in "The House of Usna," effectually alienated the sympathies of most of the founders of the Irish movement. His two plays possess undeniable atmospheric quality, and, like all the writings of "Fiona," great beauty of style. They do not seem, however, essential drama; they lean heavily, even in theory, upon the early plays of Maeterlinck. The theory which they embody was one which looked to the possibility of creating a "psychic drama," a drama of disembodied presences, a drama entirely spiritual in its content. And although he experimented to this end in his two plays, they do not, like the early plays of Yeats, who was also influenced by Maeterlinck, seem to be individual utterance, but merely the adaptation of Maeterlinck's methods to the heroic legends of Ireland.

In his prose tales Sharp was actuated by almost the same motives. He was interested in all things psychic, he held theories of ancestral memory, of "second sight," of the power of symbols, and these interests dominate his work. Old legend and curious folk-belief were the source of much of his writing, they were, in fact, the foundation upon which he raised a superstructure of speculative embroidery and delicate emotional introspection. Each of them is directed to the evocation of a definite emotional reaction, but this reaction is produced less by the content of the tale than by the manner of its setting forth. His style, delicate, tenuous, or, as he himself termed it, "mist-laden," is the most important element in his art, and is, perhaps, the cause for the brevity of his fame. For behind that fluid expression we feel that there is little consciously directed intelligence; it is prose poetry of a very high order, at its best, and at its worst it degenerates into mere toying with words and uncontrolled emotional vaporing. This quality of "fine writing" becomes almost irritating in some passages of his work, especially since it seems to serve no essential purpose other than to convey an over-sentimentalized mood.

In certain of his tales, however, those particularly which reconstruct the ancient Gaelic life, he was more successful. "Silk o' the Kine," "Enya of the Dark Eyes," "The Annir Choile," "The Fisher of Men" and "The Harping of Cravetheen" he reconstructed and built upon legend and brought out a new beauty of feeling that is distinctive of his work at its highest levels. Like Yeats, he sought to suggest the occult, the mys-

terious, the orphic element of Gaelic life, and these
moods are those which he conveys with the greatest sureness and with the most compelling beauty.
Always, however, one feels the personal element,
the fact that the eerie, orphic quality inheres less
in the old life that he was trying to reconstruct
than in his own dream of what that life may have
been.   In the final analysis Sharp's work indicates
a striving after beauty of mood for the sake purely
of that beauty.   It bears little relation to life, even
to what he himself termed spiritual life, but it does
embody the attempt to capture and to express a
beauty very different from any that had previously
graced English literature.   The final criticism of
his work is suggested in a letter written to him by
A. E.: "You know too that I think that these
alluring visions and thoughts are of little importance unless they link themselves unto our humanity.   It means only madness in the end.   I
know people whose lamps are lit and they see
wonderful things but they themselves will not pass
from vision into action.   They follow beauty only
like the dwellers in Tyre whom Ezekiel denounced,
'They have corrupted their wisdom by reason of
their brightness.'   Leaving these mystic things
aside what you say about art is quite true except

that I cannot regard art as the 'quintessential life' unless art comes to mean the art of living more than the art of the artist is." [1]

There are three outstanding figures in the Irish renascence who have employed the essay as a medium of expression. Two of them, A. E. and Yeats, are primarily poets. The third, "John Eglinton" (W. K. Magee), has concentrated all his creative energy in the production of the three slim volumes of prose that have come from his pen. Much of their work has been critical, and some controversial in character; the chief controversy in which all three have been involved was that arising from the question as to whether the way of Irish literature should be that of the national or of the cosmopolitan spirit. This discussion, since it defined many of the issues in the subsequent literary activity of the movement, has been commented upon in the chapter on the critical theories of the renascence.

The changing character of A. E.'s prose mirrors a corresponding change in his interests and preoccupations. "As I get older," he writes in an essay on Seumas O'Sullivan, "I get more songless."

[1] "William Sharp, A Memoir," by Elizabeth Sharp, Duffield and Company, New York, 1912, Vol. II, page 95.

The earlier dream-tales such as "The Mask of Apollo" (1893), "A Dream of Angus Oge" (1897), "The Story of a Star" (1894) and "The Midnight Blossom" (1894) are, like his early poems, expressions of the adventures of his spirit, communicating the interior vision that made him aware of his complex spiritual life. The vision is enmeshed in the net of faint harmonies and beautiful symbols, complex, often a little obscure, since it is intuition and emotion, rather than intellectual thought, that is seeking expression. In the two essays on "The Renewal of Youth" (1896) and "The Hero in Man" (1901) is implicit the complete statement of his philosophy. In them we have still the poet telling of his spiritual experiences, but finding also the relation of these experiences to life. "Let us get near to realities," he writes. "We read too much. . . . The soul of the modern mystic is becoming a mere hoarding-place for uncomely theories."

And in that essay on the poetry of Yeats which he calls "A Poet of Shadows" he again voices that feeling. "We, all of us, poets, artists, and musicians, who work in shadows, must sometime begin to work in substance, and why should we grieve if one labor ends and another begins? I am interested more in life than in the shadows of life, and as Ildathach grows fainter I await eagerly the revelation of the real nature of one who has built so many mansions in the heavens."

It was at about this time that Ildathach grew very faint in the mind of A. E. He had become connected with the I. A. O. S. as an organizer of rural industries, and became the editor of "The Irish Homestead,"· an agricultural journal. The spiritualistic seances in the house in Ely Place were given up, he ceased to write of his visions and spiritual intuitions, and began to write about pigs, and scientific farming, coöperative purchase and distribution, and the new polity that was to arise in Ireland. The best journalism that is being done in England today is the weekly article that A. E. writes for "The Irish Homestead." He has brought it into the homes of men who know nothing about agriculture, but who read it for its economic theory, or for the social philosophy of its editor. And he has brought it into the homes of Irish and even of American farmers whose sole interest lies in its sound agricultural doctrine. The change in essential subject brought with it a corresponding change in style. A. E. writes simply, directly, clearly, with a perfect control

over his ideas. He has become, as Dublin cap-
italists learned during the lockout of 1913, a
powerful opponent in controversy, a brilliant
satirist, and an analyst of distinct acumen. He
no longer deals with his spiritual experiences, or
weaves a beautiful texture of harmony from words.
He preaches the gospel of national regeneration,
and in "Coöperation and Nationality" this gospel
received its first ordered and logical expression.
The substance of his theory of social economy and
its effect upon Irish life will be made clear in the
following chapter. It is sufficient, however, to
say that if Irish literature has lost a poet, Irish
life has gained immeasurably in acquiring an economic and social philosopher.

But Irish literature has not wholly lost the poet
and mystic. His social theory is largely the
product of his individual philosophy, and the poet
and essayist frequently comes to the surface. An
occasional essay upon "Art and Literature" or
upon "The Poetry of James Stephens" or the
other interests to which he has at various times
given his heart reveals the fact that there has been
no fundamental disjunction between the poet and
the philosopher. If the poetry of his more mature
years has less of the yearning for the infinite, and

is closer to the life of his country as he has come to
know it than that of his youth, it is only the result of the return upon life foreshadowed in the
passages quoted above. A change in manner,
though not in feeling, has likewise come into his
painting. His earliest pictures sought to express
the visions that, coming out of nowhere, brought
him into relation with the larger spiritual life of
which he has been the only prophet in our contemporary literature. Today the visions appear
in his painting less purely as vision and veiled by
the beauty that he has found in the mysterious
landscape of Ireland.

The poet and the seer have come forward only
recently. The poet, jealous of the honor of his
nation, proud in his ideals, out of an austere faith
and flaming passion rebuked a traducer of his
land. In A. E.'s "Ulster—An Open Letter to
Rudyard Kipling" (1912), there is the finest in-
vective literature that has appeared since Steven-
son's "Father Damien." [1] And the seer wrote,
at the beginning of the war, "The Spiritual Conflict," perhaps the most religious and spiritual

[1] Both "Ulster" and "The Spiritual Conflict" are included in the volume of A. E.'s collected prose: "Imaginations and Reveries," Maunsel and Company, Dublin, 1915.

contribution to the literature of the Great War. It has for its thesis the following quotation,which might well serve as a phrase epitomizing the whole content of A. E.'s work: "The universe exists for the purpose of the soul."

William Butler Yeats has been the most prodigal and the most prolific essayist of the renascence. He has written upon the art of the theater, upon the philosophy of Shelley's poetry, upon folk-lore, upon magic and symbolism, upon painting, upon dramatic diction, upon "decadent" literature, upon Ireland in modern art, and upon other subjects too numerous to mention. Much of this writing has been done to serve an immediate purpose, to set right a wrong, to clarify the ideals of the literary workers of the renascence, or to interpret some art, or writing, or philosophy, which had taken a firm hold upon his imagination. Much of it, therefore, is merely temporary in its interest, or valuable only as an indication of his intellectual and emotional growth as a critic and artist. Some part of it has expressed a great deal of his philosophy of art and theory of life, and that, for the most part, has already been discussed in these pages. The lack of humanitarian sympathy in his early work, which was deplored by William

Larminie, has gradually disappeared, and in his
later essays Yeats has begun to voice a feeling
that the function of art is to celebrate life. This
interest in what may be called realism was doubt-
less greatly influenced by the art of Synge, and it
is something more than coincidence that the followers of Yeats, originally an idealist and a mystic, are realists in their art, while the followers of
A. E., who deserted poetry and mysticism for
economic reform, are the sole survivors of the
idealistic philosophy of the movement. Yeats
no longer hopes for a regenerated Ireland; he has
said that Ireland has become, like England, "a
nation of hucksters, counting ha'pence from a
greasy till."   But the young men of the I. A. O. S.
are full of the hope of an Ireland reborn, and
gradually they have begun to bring their dream
to realization.

"John Eglinton" and T. M. Kettle have much
in common. Both have been at variance with
the leaders of the renascence upon many points.
Both are cosmopolitan in their interests and in
their theories, both believe that Ireland will become Ireland only by becoming European. The
latter is a politician, a sociologist, and a man of
letters. He has lately been the author, with

Stephen Gwynn, of "Songs of the Irish Brigade."
His essays, collected in a volume entitled "The
Day's Burden" (1910), deal with politics, literature and economics, and include the first study
of the work of Otto Effertz, the syndicalist, to be
written in English.

"John Eglinton" has concerned himself less
with problems distinctively social or distinctively
literary than with the discussion of ideas from a
philosophic standpoint. He has been the one
writer of the renascence to advocate the employment of philosophic criticism in relation to its
problems, and he has stood always for clear thinking rather than for obscure emotionalism. Peculiarly enough, he is, if we define his philosophic
outlook, a mystic. But he has proven himself
the most logically analytical thinker that the
movement in Ireland has produced. His prose,
being the expression of an acute intelligence, is
clear, penetrating, and brilliant. Moreover, it
does not lack the beauty of phrasing and the grace
of manner that one looks for in all contemporary
Irish writing. Its beauties are concealed by the
ruggedness with which it parallels his thought,
but the "Two Essays on the Remnant" (1896)
and "Pebbles from a Brook" (1901) contain

some of the finest writing, from the point of view of expression, that has been done in contemporary letters. Yeats pointed out that the first mentioned possessed unusual "orchestral harmonies." They do. But the fundamentally important thing about "John Eglinton's" writing as a whole is not its "style," but the ideas to which it has given expression. For these the readers must go to his books. And they are among the really valuable contributions to modern thought.

CHAPTER VI

MOVEMENTS FOR SOCIAL AND ECONOMIC REFORM.
HOME RULE, SINN FEIN, THE IRISH VOLUN-
TEERS, THE REBELLION

THE two chief movements for social and economic reform in Ireland, the Gaelic League
and the Irish Agricultural Organization Society,
although absolutely distinct from each other, are
possessed fundamentally of a common aim, the
regeneration of Irish life. The Gaelic League
has striven for the preservation and rehabilitation of national culture on the basis of language;
the coöperative movement has attempted, by
applying sound social and economic doctrine to
the problems of agricultural life, a regeneration
that in its methods and in its results has been no
less spiritual than material.

The Gaelic League was founded in 1893 by Dr.
Douglas Hyde with the assistance of Father
Eugene O'Growney, David Comyn, O'Neill Rus-
sell and John MacNeill. At the outset the
League disclaimed any religious or political predi-

lections; its sole objects were the preservation of
Irish as the racial language, the study of ancient
Irish literature, and the creation of a modern
literature in modern Irish. The League at first
met with great opposition from those who felt
that it would tend to foster differences between
Ireland and England and foment a propaganda
for home rule. It soon became obvious that the
League was entirely without the sphere of religious or political controversy, for Orangemen and
Nationalists, Catholic and Protestant met and
worked together at the reconstitution of the Irish
language in perfect amity. Conditions were
hardly favorable to the propaganda instituted by
Dr. Hyde. In the west, where a remnant of the
population employed Irish colloquially, the language had been sinking into disrepute; it had, to a
very great extent, been banished from the schools,
and even where it had not been omitted from the
educational program the conditions imposed had
made it impossible to attract many students.
The League realized that it was immediately
necessary to preserve the use of Irish in the districts where it was still spoken, for a dead language
cannot possibly be revived. It therefore chose
the western counties as a primary field, and grad-

ually organized classes throughout the country.
These classes drew their recruits chiefly from the
artisans and peasants; the League grew by leaps
and bounds, forming classes in England, and
branches in the United States and in South America. Local, provincial, and national festivals and
competitions were organized, in which prizes were
awarded for recitation, singing, dancing, literary
production, and musical composition. The
League undertook to publish Irish literature in
the Irish language, and possesses two periodical
organs, "An Claideamh Soluis" and "Irisleabhar
na Gaedhilge." There have been off-shoots from
the parent society, such as Inghinidhe na hEireann
(The Daughters of Erin) and the political separatist
league, Cuman na nGaedheal. It has also forced
the adoption of Irish into the curriculum of the
schools under certain conditions, founded a school
for higher Celtic study, and has played an important role in the struggle with Trinity College for
the foundation of a national university under the
control of Irish scholars, as it has in the constant
wrangle over the composition of the school boards.
Until very recently political considerations were
absent in the League; political jobbery, however,
finally entered, and Dr. Hyde was forced from the

presidency. Just what the future will bring it is difficult to say. What the League has done, however, is to reconstitute Irish as a living, and in part as a national, language, to revive the study of national literature, and to produce a literature in modern Irish. It has revived some of the ancient communal arts and sports, and thus in a measure begun the reconstruction of social life. In so doing it has exerted a profound influence upon the contemporary renascence in Ireland, not only in literature, the arts, and political thought, but in the crystallization of a social consciousness.

The coöperative movement in agriculture, as the I. A. O. S. is generally known, has established reforms of a more widely extended character and of far greater material importance in their social and economic aspect than those of any other constructive agency in Ireland. The movement owes its inception and its fundamental direction to the vision and to the energy of one man, Sir Horace Plunkett. Horace Plunkett—he had not then received his title—had been a rancher in the western United States, chiefly in Nebraska, for ten years when, in 1889, he returned to Ireland for a visit. He was a man of independent means, a member of the Dunsany family, a Protestant and a unionist in politics, a successful man of affairs, and the possessor of many interests in the United States which he still retains, and to which he pays an annual visit of inspection. In the States he had witnessed the tendency toward industrial combination whereby many small industrial units, unsuccessful in their mutual competition, had combined, eliminated useless waste, and in their new capacity had become economically successful. When he returned to Ireland he found a nation of small farmers, unsatisfactory conditions of land tenure, primitive methods of agriculture, a rate of emigration that threatened to drain the land completely, widespread poverty and indebtedness, and few returns from the energy expended upon the land. He found the government constantly appealed to for aid, but doing little beyond the periodical appointment of boards of inquiry into the various phases of agricultural discontent, and occasionally applying various remedies that seemed never to alleviate the suffering of the farmers. He found the farmers almost constantly laboring under a burden of debt to the "gombeen man," as the Irish call the local usurer. The gombeen man was usually the local storekeeper, and often the local political

boss. Indebtedness to him meant continual purchase from him of the necessaries of life at a
greatly enhanced value, and the sale to him of
whatever agricultural products he chose to buy
at a constantly diminishing rate, so that the burden of debt invariably increased, and the farm, no
matter how good the crops, was forever run at a
loss. Sir Horace Plunkett saw these conditions
which had obtained almost everywhere in Ireland
since the time of the great famine, but not content with mere lamentation, he determined that
they should be rectified, without government aid,
by the farmers themselves. He was in no sense
a trained economist nor a specialist in agriculture,
but he had vision and an infinite persuasion with
which to expound it. The first people whom he
persuaded were R. A. Anderson, who was then
the supervisor of the tenants of Lord Castledown,
and Father Thomas Finlay, a young Jesuit priest
who had studied in Germany. The three of
them set to work spreading the gospel of coöperation. By 1894 the movement had become too
large to be successfully carried further by individuals, and the Irish Agricultural Organization
Society was formed. Opposition was not lacking,
chiefly on the part of the gombeen men, who or-

ganized for self protection and entrusted their political interests to T. W. Russell. In 1897 the I. A. O. S. required the services of an additional organizer, and Sir Horace asked William Butler Yeats whether he knew of anyone for the position. Yeats spoke of a mystic poet, who had addressed the Sunday crowds at Bray Head, who was deeply versed in the lore of mysticism, and the leader of the Hermetic Society, but who also happened to be an accountant at Pim's in Dublin. The visionary whom he recommended had published poetry and prose in various magazines under the pseudonym of A. E. Luckily, Sir Horace persuaded A. E. into the movement, and sent him off touring the country on his bicycle as an organizer for the society. After a few years of organizing, he was appointed assistant secretary, and in 1905 became editor of "The Irish Homestead," the official organ of the I. A. O. S. This little excursus into the history of the society is prerequisite to any discussion of its fundamental ideas because although coöperation, as a practical issue, was the idea of Sir Horace Plunkett, the superstructure of a social philosophy has been raised by A. E.[1]

[1] Three books are especially valuable in explanation of

The remedy that Sir Horace proposed seemed
so simple that the majority of people laughed at
it. Agriculture, he held, is a science, an industry, and a life. His slogan was "Better farming,
better business, better living." Stripped to its
bare essentials, his plan was that the Irish farmers
should combine to their own advantage. The
small farmer, competing with his neighbor, is
always at a disadvantage. He cannot buy expensive machinery, his credit is bad, he knows
little about the modern scientific methods of
agrarian industry. Such was the condition of
the average Irish farmer when Sir Horace began
the coöperative campaign. He showed them
how it was possible, by combining and coöperating, to purchase the requisite expensive machinery
for the use of the community, to buy supplies,
also for the use of the community, at wholesale
rates, to sell his products, in combination with
those of his neighbors, at retail prices, since in
combination a group of farmers could themselves

the coöperative movement: "Ireland in the New Century,"
by Sir Horace Plunkett, Macmillan; "Coöperation and
Nationality," by George W. Russell (A. E.), Maunsel and
Co. Ltd., Dublin, 1912; and "The United Irishwomen, Their
Place, Work and Ideals," by Horace Plunkett, Ellice Pilk-
ington, and A. E., Maunsel, 1912.

regulate the selling price. He also showed them that, although their individual credit was bad, as a community coöperating for the benefit of all their members, their credit was good. He inaugurated credit societies, Raiffeisen Banks, agricultural societies, poultry societies, home industry societies, and various miscellaneous groups, such as those of the bee-keepers, the flax-growers, and the bacon-curers. He also formed the Irish Agricultural Wholesale Society, which is responsible for the distribution of products, and another society which purchases machinery for the coöperative associations. This was "Better business." But "Better farming" was the primary factor in his program. This, too, was accomplished. A group of agricultural experts were impressed into the service of the society, studies were made of the most modern methods of agriculture, and the knowledge obtained was disseminated among the farmers by itinerant teachers and organizers. All this work was undertaken by the various societies acting through the central controlling agency of the I. A. O. S.

Statistics seldom make interesting reading. But the statistics of the I. A. O. S. convey, in concrete form, some impression of the results of their labors.[1] During the first year of its operation, the single coöperative society did a total business of $21,815.00. The statistics for 1913 have been computed as follows.

Societies	Number	Membership	Business
Dairy (Creameries)	341	41,106	$12,623,105.00
Auxiliary	89		
Agricultural	193	19,970	881,505.00
Credit	235	20,211	276,451.00
Poultry	18	5,294	241,680.00
Home Industries	18	1,212	15,105.00
Miscellaneous (bees, bacon etc.)	27	9,492	684,085.00
Pig and Cattle Supply	52	1,730	
Flax	10	406	5,015.00
Federations	2	231	1,935,990.00
Totals	895	104,702	$16,665,990.00

In conjunction with these figures one may read the following account of the work of the I. A. O. S. by A. E.: "The dairy societies have released the farmer from the bondage to the butter merchant and proprietor, and given back to him the control

[1] These statistics are quoted from an article on "The Farmer's Fight—The Example of the Irish Farmers," by Charles Edward Russell, in "Pearson's Magazine," for September, 1915.

,of the processes of manufacture and sale. In the credit societies farmers join together, and, creating by their union a greater security than any of them could offer individually, they are able to get money to finance their farming operations at very low rates. The joint stock banks lend money to these societies on wholesale terms, letting them retail it again among their members. Generally speaking, it has been found possible to borrow money at from three to four per cent. and to lend it for productive purposes at the popular rate of one penny a month for every pound employed. The trust auctioneer's methods, the gombeen man's methods, cannot stand this competition. The poultry societies collect the eggs of their members, they grade and pack them properly, and market them through their own agencies. The flax societies erect or hire scutch mills and see that the important work of scutching the flax is performed with the requisite care. The agricultural societies purchase seeds, implements, fertilizers, feeding stuffs, and agricultural requirements for their members. Many of them hold thousands of pounds' worth of machinery too expensive for the individual farmer to buy. The societies buy their requirements at wholesale prices and insure good quality. The home industries' societies have made hopeful beginnings with lace, crochet, embroidery and rug-making to provide work for country girls. . . . The societies in Ireland are losing their specialized character, their limitation of objects to this purpose or that, and are more and more assuming a character which can only be described by calling them general purposes' societies. The successful dairy society begins to take up the work of an agricultural, poultry or credit society in addition to the work for which the farmers were originally organized in the district. It is gradually absorbing into one large well managed association all the rural business connected with agriculture in each parish. The societies are controlled by committees elected by the members, and in a decade or so, instead of the dislocation and separation of interests which has been so disastrous in its effects, instead of innumerable petty businesses all striving for their own rather than for the general welfare, there will be in each parish one large association able to pay well for expert management, with complete control over all processes of purchase, manufacture and sale, and run by the farmers with the energy of self interest. These

district associations are rapidly linking themselves
on to large federations for purchase and sale, which
again are controlled by representatives of the societies, and through these the farmers are able to
act powerfully in the market. They become their
own middlemen. All the links between production on the farm and sale to the consumer are
controlled by the agriculturist. These societies,
their federations, and the I. A. O. S. form the
nucleus, and a very strong nucleus, for a vast
farmers' trade union, ready to protect their interests, to help them socially, politically, and
economically."

What, then, of the final words of Sir Horace
Plunkett's slogan, "Better living"? He himself
has written thus: "Both the practice and the
business of farming have been revolutionized by
bringing science into the one and modern business
methods—chiefly methods of combination—into
the other. The country workers must do with
their industry and with its business just what the
town workers have been forced to do with theirs.
And when all this is done, if the domestic and social life of the country does not advance with its
economic life, all but the dullards will fly to the
town." That phase of the program has been

undertaken by the United Irishwomen, an association similar to the I. A. O. S., and represented therein, which organizes the social life of the rural communities. It is coöperative, and its work is not that of a benevolent autocracy, nor that of a superior power charitably inclined, but it is conceived and carried out by the women of the new rural civilization themselves. It devotes itself to agricultural industries, to domestic economy, to social and intellectual development. It brings to the rural communities things as far apart as the latest methods of accounting and the latest theories of community sanitation. It organizes lectures, clubs, community halls wherein community festivities take place, district nursing, concerts, education, and home industries. It does this not impersonally, but with an absolute personal connection with the community, for the associated communities give it its life. And in doing so it is working out a social philosophy not even hoped for by the founder of the movement at its inception, twenty-six years ago.

This is the social economy of A. E. as it is being realized in Ireland today. He it was who saw that if Ireland was to have a national life, that life must be of its own creation. He saw the

futility of governmental regulation, the huge impersonality of legislative enactment superimposed
upon a people by a body of men with no knowledge
of actually existing conditions.   He saw that society, and particularly rural society, did not exist
when the Land Acts provided for tenant purchase.
He knew that such a social order must necessarily
be built up, and he threw his force into the cooperative movement.   It has been a bloodless
revolution, but a revolution nevertheless.   Out
of a nation of farmers whose relation to the holders
of the land, in 1889, was that of the feudal serf
to his overlord, he has witnessed the crystallization of a nation of farmers combined and coöperating, successful, happy, developing a civilization
and a nationality of their own.   "Nature," he has
written, "has no intention of allowing her divine
brood, made in the image of Deity, to dwindle
away into a crew of little, feeble, feverish city folk.
She has other and more grandiose futures before
humanity if ancient prophecy and our deepest,
most spiritual, intuitions have any truth in them."
Therefore he has fulfilled his vision by laying the
foundations of a rural civilization and a nationality
upon the bed-rock of communal effort and communal consciousness.

The government, however, had not been inactive in the meanwhile. Its social and economic program for Ireland involved three distinct phases. First in importance was the Land Purchase Act, second, the relief of conditions in the "congested districts," which is really a special problem connected with land tenure, and finally, the creation of a Department of Agriculture and Technical Instruction.

The earliest land purchase act was that drafted by Lord Ashbourne, and passed in 1885. It provided that if any landlord wished to sell his estate to his tenants, the Imperial Treasury would advance the whole of the purchase money upon certain guarantees, the purchaser to repay the amount in forty-nine annuities, each equal to four per cent. of the purchase price. Such agreements were binding only when ratified by the Land Commission. The government appropriated ten millions of pounds to the promulgation of the act. In 1891, and again in 1896, the money appropriated was exhausted and new acts were passed. That of 1891 complicated the machinery of purchase, and the following act was no great improvement. These acts stemmed the tide of purchase, and in 1903 it was deemed necessary to provide further incentive. The result was the Wyndham Act, prepared by the Chief Secretary for Ireland, which provided for an optional land purchase of all estates, whether entailed or not, whose proprietors desired to sell, the estate to be sold as a whole to tenants acting coöperatively. All transactions are under the control of the Estates Commissioners, who must pass upon each case without comment if the contracting parties agree to fix the purchase price within certain "zones." The tenant, although paying a smaller annuity under this system, must continue paying for a longer duration of time. The Commissioners can buy estates with a view to resale, especially if these estates are what is known as "congested." The expenses of operating the act are almost entirely charged against Irish funds.

The "congested districts" are chiefly in the west, Connemara, Connaught, and Kerry. They are a survival of the clearances which took place after the great famine, and the institution of grazing in what formerly had been land cultivated by tenant farmers. Excessive subdivisions and the turning of the land over to grazing have been responsible for this "congestion." A "congested district" is one in which most of the good land is

given over to grazing, and the barren soil that remains is allotted in infinitely small holdings to the
tenants, who live in mud hovels, and whose holdings are "uneconomic" in that they do not produce
enough to support life. To remedy this condition
the Board was formed and voted a grant of money.
It buys estates, erects cottages, and allots the land
in economic holdings to the tenants who purchase
it. It encourages the fishing industry, and relieves
the congestion by removing tenants to other por-
tions of the country where vacant land is available.
It works in conjunction with the I. A. O. S. and
with the Department of Agriculture, and it sub-
sidizes industries in the process of formation. It
has, however, no power of compulsory expropria-
tion of the landlord, which is the greatest hindrance
to land reform in Ireland.

The Department of Agriculture and Technical
Instruction owes its inception to Sir Horace
Plunkett, who in 1895, as a member of Parliament,
formed a "Recess Committee" which occupied
itself with an inquiry as to the best methods of
state aid to agricultural industries obtaining in
other countries. Their report formed the basis of
an act passed in 1899, which established the department, with Sir Horace at its head. It received

a grant of two hundred thousand pounds capital, and an annual income of one hundred and sixty-six thousand pounds which, with the exception of five thousand pounds, is drawn from Irish sources. Its purpose was to develop agriculture, and to furnish technical instruction in agriculture and related industries. It took over the management of the Royal College of Science, the Metropolitan School of Art, and the Science and Art Museum in Dublin. It opened various schools and agricultural stations throughout the country. It subsidized the I. A. O. S., to which Sir Horace gave his salary, and it coöperated with local authorities throughout Ireland in its program of economic reform. But seven years after its constitution, a change in party removed Sir Horace from his position as Vice President, and the new incumbent, Mr. T. W. Russell, the supporter of the gombeen men and a foe to the coöperative movement, reduced the grant to the I. A. O. S., and weakened the efficiency of the department as a constructive force in Irish economic life. It does, however, through its itinerant teachers, through its bulletins and the work of its agricultural and technical experts, influence reform in Ireland.

These five agencies have to a very great extent

revived the economic life of Ireland and established it upon a firm foundation. The chief concern of the government has been the land question, since organized opposition has concentrated with greater frequency upon that than upon any other phase of the situation in Ireland. And for such concentration there has been good cause. With the exception of Belfast and the district immediately surrounding it, Ireland is primarily an agricultural nation. It has always been a nation of small farmers. Had these small farmers possessed the absolute control of their land, self interest would have led to its cultivation, to the erection of homes, and to the investment of whatever capital they had in improvements of a reproductive nature the benefits of which would have been guaranteed to them by the permanence of their tenure. This, however, has never been the case. The curse of absentee landlordism held the greater part of Ireland in its grip, the rights of the landlord in the summary eviction of tenants for non-payment of rent, the provision that improvements of whatever nature became the property of the landlord without compensation to the evicted tenant, the insecurity of tenure even where the rent was promptly met, the difficulty for all these

reasons of obtaining credit, the average high rate of
rent and the primitive methods of agriculture employed all combined not only to deprive the
peasantry of all ambition, but to make any sound
rural economy impossible for them.   After the
great famine, and the clearances, the situation became still more acute, and after the evictions of
1879, an agrarian rebellion broke out which continued sporadically for thirteen years.   The Land
League, and its successor, the Ladies' Land
League, inaugurated a campaign of retaliation
which began with a boycott and ended with the
anarchy and terror spread by the "Ribbonmen"
and "Moonlighters."   In the meanwhile, the
economic difficulty had become a political issue,
and as is usually the case under such circumstances,
had in no wise been solved.   Finally Gladstone
influenced legislative enactment which provided
for a complicated and expensive judicial machinery to determine tenant rights.   A policy of
"dual ownership" came into being, whereby the
landlord actually retained possession of the land,
while the tenant was invested with certain rights
which he might sell or otherwise dispose of.   Fixity
of tenure, however, was not guaranteed him, although he came into possession of the other two

rights for which there had been so much agitation, fair rent, and free sale. The system of dual ownership, however, proved to be an uneconomic solution, for the landlord refused to invest capital in his estates, desiring merely to draw his rents from them, and the tenant refused to make the necessary improvements lest the rent be raised after he had done so because of the increased value of the land. Moreover, the force of competition exerted itself in the purchase of tenant rights, the right to occupation of the land, and because of certain peculiar provisions of the legislation, the peasant found himself in the position of having to pay many times the actual rental value of the land in order to occupy it and pay rent to the landlord for the privilege.

Ireland still looked to the government for a solution of its difficulties, however, and a partial solution was effected, not without criticism, by the various land purchase acts. These in theory effected the transfer of the land from the aristocracy to the peasantry, and such a transfer has been inaugurated in practice. A corresponding transfer of political power was effected by Gerald Balfour's Local Government Act, passed in 1898. This provided for a general reform in local administration, placing it in the hands of the county councils, who are elected by a wide franchise to which women are admitted, but clergymen excluded. The county councils can send delegates to the general council of county councils, which has little power of any nature, and is supervised by the Local Government Board, controlled by the Castle.

The effect of all this legislation has been to destroy the old rural social and economic systems. The transfer of the land to the peasant disposed of the old economic relation between tenant and landlord, and the transfer of political power effected a change in the proportional weight of class influence, so that the peasant found himself in the position of a landowner with certain political powers and duties directly devolving upon him. And he found himself in this position without any previous experience in either his new economic or political capacity. If the small agriculturalist was to remain, economically, an individualist, capital was an immediate requisite. This the purchaser of land did not often possess, and if outside capital were called in, the probable result would have been the creation of a trust, and the peasant would have been in no better condition than before. The middleman, who had operated against the farmer while he was yet a tenant, could operate against him in the same fashion now that he was a proprietor. What was urgently necessary was the creation of a new social and economic system, and this the coöperative movement undertook. It has carried it through successfully both with the aid of the state and without that aid. And today, as has been said, a new social order and a new national life is coming into being in Ireland. And this has its basis in a new kind of rural civilization, in which Ireland has become the world's teacher.

The political history of Ireland since the Act of Union has been a story of continuous struggle for home rule, a story in which internal dissension, factional strife and disaffection of all kinds have operated against the achievement of any permanent reform. In its more recent history, since the defeat of Gladstone's Home Rule Bill in 1893, there have been four political philosophies advanced. The Nationalist party has been declared for home rule, home rule meaning the creation of an Irish Parliament at Dublin subservient to the Imperial Parliament at Westminster. The Unionists have declared against home rule in any form. Between the Unionists and the Nationalists, and descried by both, there has been a group of radical conservatives who put forward a plan that seemed like conciliation to the Nationalists and like rank heresy to the Unionists. This plan was put forward in 1904 by the Irish Reform Association, a group of Unionist landlords and wealthy men of the middle class, under the title of "devolution," a name given it by Lord Dunraven, the president of the association. This provided that such bills of a purely local and those of a semipublic nature as Parliament would allow, and all private bills, should devolve upon an Irish deliberative chamber the constitution of which was left undecided. It provided also for the creation of an Irish Financial Council of twenty-four members, half of whom were to be appointed by the Lord Lieutenant, and the other half elected by the people. The function of this council was to prepare and control the Irish budget, and to dispose of such funds as Parliament granted. The rights of Parliament were, however, safeguarded in all cases. This plan fell through, having incurred the enmity of both principal parties.[1]

[1] It seems, at the present writing (May 16th, 1916) as if the second provision of the devolution policy will be inaugurated temporarily, until the conclusion of the war and the promulgation of home rule. Mr. Asquith, on his journey to Dublin after the April insurrection, is thought to favor its adoption.

The fourth wing in Irish politics has been composed of the Sinn Fein party, inheritors of the traditions of John Mitchel and of the Fenians, whose philosophy has been one of passive resistance, and more recently, of physical force. The movement was organized in 1903 by Arthur Griffith, a brilliant young journalist who advocated the adoption by Ireland of the policy instituted by Ferencz Déak during Hungary's struggle for autonomy from 1849 to 1867. The chief feature of this policy was a national boycott. The Hungarians, under the leadership of Déak, refused to send representatives to the joint parliament, refused to pay taxes unless they were levied and collected by Hungarian officials, and instituted an educational and administrative system independent of that of the government, and extended this national boycott to their economic life, refusing all trade relations with Austria. By 1867 this policy brought about a practical autonomy for Hungary. Griffith, in seeking to apply it to Ireland, advocated a similar passive revolution. Unfortunately he ran foul of both the political parties and the Church, and the movement, which commenced by being non-partisan, adopted a party platform, and succeeded in electing candidates to various offices in the local government.

Their program involved certain very radical features. They wished the local government, or that part of it which is controlled by the Irish electorate, to sit as a Parliament in Dublin, and together with the Irish contingent in the House of Commons, pass laws and recommend policies for adoption by Ireland. This proposed parliament would, of course, have no constitutional standing, but would be upheld as a moral authority; their enactments, although having no effect as constitutional law, would have the effect of moral law. The entire Irish representation in the House of Commons were to resign from office, and no successors were to be voted for. Among the laws to be passed was one decreeing a voluntary tax of a penny to the pound, to be employed in the development of an educational system. An embargo upon the importation of all English goods was also to be passed. National courts of law, presided over by justices of the peace during the hours in which the present courts were not in session, were to be established, and the present courts boycotted. Irish was to be the official language of the de facto administration. The English army and navy were to be boycotted, and the government civil service and constabulary also. Finally, certain economic re-

forms were to go into operation, of which agricultural coöperation was the chief.

The leaders of Sinn Fein gathered a large following, which they organized in secret societies
throughout Ireland. They published a weekly
paper called at first "The United Irishmen," and
later by the name of the movement, Sinn Fein,
which, literally translated from the Gaelic, means
"Ourselves Alone" (ourselves for ourselves). In
this journal appeared some of the best writing
produced by the literary renascence, and its contributors numbered practically every important
writer that has been mentioned in these pages.
The Sinn Fein movement was in no respect a class
movement, and although it drew its vigor from
the adherence of the young intellectuals, it was a
popular movement with a popular following, the
first of whose tenets was the fundamental equality
of all men and their moral equivalence in the struggle to bring about Irish freedom. The movement,
in theory at least, may be compared to that of the
I. A. O. S. The philosophy fundamental in both
has been that of Irish regeneration by Irishmen
through coöperative action and without external
aid. The point wherein the movements have dif-
fered is that Sinn Fein has desired a complete sever-

ance from all things English, believing that Ireland must achieve constitutional independence by a renunciation of all dependence, economic, administrative, intellectual, upon England, while the I. A. O. S. has labored, without any ulterior political philosophy, to establish a new social and economic order.

In 1913, under the direction of the Irish Transport Union, a strike of farm-laborers was organized which threatened to cripple the work of the cooperative movement. At the same time, a strike was organized in Dublin. In Dublin the strike became a lockout inaugurated by the federated employers, who proceeded to starve out the strikers. James Larkin organized the workers to resist the methods of the employers. In this he was supported by Sinn Fein, and by a group of young poets and writers who were revolutionary in their thinking. Larkin himself is a syndicalist, a fiery orator, and possesses a large personal following, which he brought into the Sinn Fein movement. Not only the whole of Ireland, but most of Great Britain was agitated by the horror of the situation in Dublin. A monster meeting was organized at Albert Hall in London, at which George Bernard Shaw and A. E., who had been active in the cause of the workers, both spoke.

Finally, the back of the lockout was broken, and both the coöperative movement and Sinn Fein had gained adherents by the stand which they had taken. Larkin and James Connolly, a labor leader and author, joined the latter movement, and the doctrines of Sinn Fein began to take on a syndicalist tone.

In the meanwhile the Home Rule bill had been discussed in the House. The radical Unionist forces and the Orange associations of Ulster threatened sedition if Home Rule became an accomplished fact. Organizers were sent from England to Ulster to foment the feeling against the bill. By 1911, a provisional government for Ulster with Sir Edward Carson at its head, had been arranged for. The government negotiated with Sir Edward Carson, but received no assurances. Money was subscribed to finance the rebellion in Ulster, and arms were imported unhindered by the British government. Then the Home Rule bill was passed. Sir Edward Carson refused any further negotiations with the British government, and troops were sent into Ulster. This was in 1914. The King intervened after troops had been sent, and several changes were made in the personnel of the commanding staff. Civil war threatened to break out at any moment.

Then, when it seemed that by complete inactivity, the government had repudiated its promise to uphold the law, the Irish Volunteers, who had been organized in December, 1913, began to import arms into Ireland. John Redmond, at the instigation of Mr. Asquith and the ministry, had taken control of the Volunteers, who thus became identified with the Nationalist party. The government sought to prevent the importation of arms into Dublin, although allowing, and even conniving in, their importation into Ulster. Soldiers were sent to Dalkey, a suburb of Dublin, to prevent the landing of arms. On their way there, as was natural, they attracted a crowd of men, women and children. Some few rowdies took the opportunity to throw stones at the troops. The troops, just as they had during the strike of 1913, fired on the crowd, killing several women and children. A mutiny broke out among the garrison at Camp Curragh, near Dublin. And just then the Great War beat down upon the world.

In June, 1914, the Irish Volunteers published the following manifesto:—

"*Fellow Countrymen,*
It is close upon seven months since the Irish Volunteers were called into being by a manifesto issued on

the 29th November, 1913, in the name of the Provisional Body, who now make this further appeal to
the courage and patriotism of Irishmen.

The time is now opportune. To that first appeal a
splendid response has been given by the youth and
manhood of Ireland.

The call to Irishmen to form an army of national
defence against aggression, from whatever quarter it
might come, and to take upon themselves the defence
of those rights and liberties common to all the people
of Ireland, has not fallen on deaf ears or cold hearts.

The right of a free people to carry arms in defence of
their freedom is an elementary part of political liberty.
The denial of that right is a denial of political liberty
and consistent only with a despotic form of government. They have rights who dare maintain them.

The demand of the Irish people is unmistakable.
They demand this elementary right of free men—the
right to place arms in the hands of the organized and
disciplined defenders of their liberty.

Ireland today possesses an army of men actuated
by a common spirit of patriotism, daily acquiring and
applying habits of disciplined and concerted action,
and rapidly fitting themselves to bear arms.

We denounce as hostile to our liberty, civic as well
as national, the denial of this right.

And, further, since the action of the Government
places in the way of Irishmen favorable to a national
autonomy obstacles which admittedly are inoperative
in the case of those opposed to the policy of Irish self

government, we urge and demand, through every representative voice in Ireland, the immediate withdrawal of the Proclamation prohibiting the import of arms into Ireland.

We are glad to recognize that the time has come when the members of the Irish Parliamentary Party, with Mr. John Redmond at its head, have been able, owing to the development of the Irish Volunteer organization on sound and well-defined national lines, to associate themselves by public declaration with a work which the nation has spontaneously taken in hand. Their accession is all the more welcome since, from the outset of the Irish Volunteer movement, we have made it our constant aim to bring about a whole and sincere unity of the Irish people on the ground of national freedom.   In that spirit, too, we look forward with eager hope to the day when the minority of our fellow-countrymen, still apparently separated from us in affection, will be joined hand in hand with the majority, in a union within which the rights and liberties common to all the people of Ireland will be sacred to all, and will be a trust to be defended by the arms and lives of all Irishmen.

> Eoin MacNeill,
> L. J. Kettle,
> *Hon. Secs.*
> *Provisional Executive.*"

On September 19th, 1914, the Home Rule bill was signed and became binding law, but its operation was postponed until after the duration of the war. In the meanwhile, John Redmond attempted to utilize the Irish Volunteers in recruiting for the English army. The Volunteers then became an organization existing for purely national purposes. They disclaimed Redmond, and went ahead with their preparations.

In May of last year, Sir Edward Carson, who had been in open rebellion against the Imperial Government, was appointed attorney general, and became a member of the Cabinet. No greater farce, from the point of view of Ireland, could have possibly come about. Either the government entrusted the prosecution of the law to an acknowledged law-breaker, or, if Sir Edward were not a criminal, the government had openly connived with the uprisings in Belfast.

The marching of armed Ulster Volunteers through Belfast, and the meeting there of a provisional government; the killing of four people and wounding of sixty others by troops in Dublin, in an attempt to prevent the landing of arms; the suspension of the Home Rule bill; the appointment of Sir Edward Carson as a minister; the refusal of the English government to permit the emigration of Irishmen of military age, and the

illiberal prosecution of the "Defense of the Realm"
Act in Ireland convinced the young Irishmen that
England's promises to Ireland were invalid.

What happened then is history too recent to
require discussion.

A revolution took place in Ireland. Fighting
obtained in Dublin from April 21st to May 1st.
Sir Roger Casement, who at the outbreak of war
had gone to the United States, repudiating his
British title, and from there to Berlin, landed at
Tralee, and was promptly captured by the British
and taken to London as a traitor. A provisional
government was declared in Ireland, with P. H.
Pearse as provisional president of the Irish Republic. Troops were hastened to Dublin from
England, and a gunboat came up the Liffey and
shelled Liberty Hall, the headquarters of the
Sinn Fein movement. On April 30th, a proclamation advising all rebels to surrender was issued by
the provisional president, P. H. Pearse. The
leaders surrendered the following day, and over a
thousand prisoners were taken. Fourteen of the
rebel leaders were shot in Dublin Castle yard as
traitors. Countess Markievicz, the sister of Miss
Eva Gore-Booth, the poetess, was ordered to hard
penal servitude for life. Thomas MacDonagh,

poet, critic and playwright, P. H. Pearse, lawyer,
Gaelic scholar and head master of St. Enda's
School, F. Sheeby Skeffington, author and lec-
turer, James Connolly, labor leader and author of
a notable economic study, "Labor in Irish History," and Joseph Plunkett, poet, were all shot.
Professor Eoin MacNeill, of the National University, a notable Gaelic scholar, was also captured.

Followed the resignations of Lord Wimborne,
Lord Lieutenant of Ireland, and Augustine Bir-
rell, chief secretary. Followed also the trip of
Mr. Asquith to Dublin, and his review of the
Irish situation.

What has been accomplished? As a rebellion,
the insurrection in Ireland has been a failure. It
has not brought Ireland independence in any but
a qualified degree. It has robbed the young Ireland movement of today of many of its finest
and keenest intellects.

It was, undoubtedly, a chimeric scheme, the
expression of a dream and of an aspiration that
have never been quiescent since the Union. It
was also, to a certain extent, the expression of the
neo-Celtic philosophy as that is understood today,
seeking a refuge from life not in art, but in action.

It made heroes, and it integrated, even more strongly than before, the race consciousness that the renascence in Ireland has developed. What the final result may be, cannot, at this moment, be determined. But the rebellion, as the expression of a new "Young Ireland" movement, has been the result of one phase of the renascence that has come over Ireland during the past twenty-six years.

The period of the renascence may justly be said to close with the rebellion. What may come afterward will be the fruit reaped from the harvest that the renascence has sowed. For it has borne a new thought, a new literature, a new economy, a new social philosophy, even a new nation in Ireland.

Printed in the United States of America.